THE SAD PARADE

The Sad Parade

Prose Poems

by

PHILIP WEXLER

Adelaide Books
New York / Lisbon
2019

THE SAD PARADE
Prose Poems
By Philip Wexler

Copyright © by Philip Wexler
Cover design © 2019 Adelaide Books

Published by Adelaide Books, New York / Lisbon
adelaidebooks.org

Editor-in-Chief
Stevan V. Nikolic

All rights reserved. No part of this book may be reproduced in any manner whatsoever without written permission from the author except in the case of brief quotations embodied in critical articles and reviews.

For any information, please address Adelaide Books
at info@adelaidebooks.org
or write to:
Adelaide Books
244 Fifth Ave. Suite D27
New York, NY, 10001

ISBN: 978-1-951214-80-7

Printed in the United States of America

With love to my wife, Nancy;

my son, Jake; my mom, Yetty and

the cherished memory of my father, Will

(1930-2019)

and an affectionate pat to our dog, Gigi

Contents

Credits **11**

Adoption Criteria **13**

The Air Hose Oracle **15**

alphabetical **17**

And the Winner is ….. **18**

Andy **20**

At the Waterlily Festival **22**

The Bouncing Ball **24**

Bowing Out **26**

Bruno **29**

the bundle **32**

But Officer **34**

Cactus Poacher **36**

The Carrying Man   *38*

Churning Golden   *39*

Cluck, Cluck   *40*

Coming Clean   *42*

The Critical Bite   *44*

Disappearing   *46*

A Diva's Triumph   *48*

drinks   *50*

The Drunkards and the Meadowlark   *52*

Elizabeth   *54*

Escapades at the Beach   *56*

Exhausted   *59*

Fair Trade   *61*

A Family Tale   *62*

The Firewood   *64*

For the Erasing of Difficulties   *68*

For the Greater Good   *69*

General Kigoshi Fujiwara's Dilemma   *70*

Getting There   *72*

THE SAD PARADE

Going Up *75*

His Trembling Left Hand *77*

Hot Goods *79*

In my Impossible Dream *80*

Jowls *81*

Ken Who? *82*

The Key Thing *84*

The Last Attack upon the Wiggly Man *86*

Midge's Fortunate Detour *87*

Nothing to Speak Of *89*

Pay Dirt *91*

pillow fight *93*

Political Aspirations *95*

The Prunes' Revenge *97*

pursuit *98*

the sad parade of big candles *100*

Sick of it All *101*

A Sizeable Confrontation *103*

Sojourn to the Deep *104*

South Jersey, Pine Barrens **106**

Shoe - Fly, Don't Bother Me **109**

The Superfluity of Wings **111**

Taking a Dump in the Middle of the Night **112**

Taking Stock **115**

Teaching the Trapezoid a Lesson **118**

Time will Tell **120**

To Prepare Broth First Chop Bone **121**

To Such an End **122**

The Third Wife **123**

Utterly **125**

The Way of the Rodeo **127**

Wedding **128**

Wedding Bells **129**

We Recover Lampshades **130**

Winner Takes All **132**

About the Author **135**

Credits

Some of these poems or earlier versions thereof have been published in:

Barkeater: The Adirondack Review, Homestead Review, Thorny Locust. KYSO Flash, Poet Lore, The Prose Poem Project, Rain Dog Review.

Adoption Criteria

We are foster parents of a sort, caring for pets until they find permanent adoptive homes. The last dog in our care, a Chihuahua mix, made quite an impression on the Nippersons, a quiet retired couple who periodically scoured Europe for antique paperweights. We were certain it was a done deal despite their not making an immediate commitment. They were, of course, entitled to think over a decision this important. We were chagrined to learn that they decided against the dog, named Chitah by the previous owner who had, subsequent to an automobile accident, become bedridden and could no longer care for her. In their letter to us, the Nippersons indicated that Chitah was simply too tall. This initially struck us as an unusual, if not wholly fabricated, explanation. My husband, Jim, drafted an irate letter to them asking if that meant that their ceilings were too low. I wouldn't let him mail it. The following month they sent us a Christmas card with best regards to Chitah, who by now had found a home with a single accountant who placed no height restrictions on his pets. The Nippersons enclosed a novelty rubber paperweight with a plastic bone inside, a toy for Chitah, and went on to explain in more detail their decision not to adopt this loving pup.

It seemed that the only acceptable way for them to take their frequent transatlantic flights with a pet was for it to travel in a carrier in the cabin. That was the way they traveled with Poopy, their late lamented purebred Chihuahua, may she rest in peace. But Chitah was no Poopy and had legs up the kazoo for a Chihuahua, or so they said, and there was no way she'd be able to stand upright in their carrier, which they insisted upon, if they were ever to travel with another canine companion. They would not impose an hours long prone position on any dog of theirs, and a larger carrier would mean the dog was bound for cargo, and that would not do for the Nippersons. They were really a lovely couple and with our mutual love of animals, we vowed to keep in touch. They wrote us again in January from Warsaw with the thrilling news that they had just purchased not only a rare sixteenth century paperweight said to have been owned by Copernicus and which encased a yellow globe said, by appraisers, to represent the sun, but finally found a new pet or, more properly, pets – two dozen Japanese fighting beetles. They fit just perfectly in Poopy's old carrier. We wished them every happiness and few casualties.

The Air Hose Oracle

The Salvadorans at the car wash were diligent and scrupulous. They would report for work very early on Monday morning, long before the boss arrived or the service was open to the public, to congregate around the Air Hose. They would sweep the ground around it clean of what they didn't recognize as flower petals and fervently set to praying. Each petition harbored a very concrete wish for tangibles like a Cadillac, winning the lottery, a house in the suburbs, a divorce, or Rosalinda Cordero who brought her Toyota van in every month and would, as the spirit moved her, invite one of the boys in back, while the others sudsed up her vehicle.

Invariably, a hiss, emanating from the Air Hose, would cause them to pause in their prayers. An objective observer would conclude it was a pinhole leak. They listened with great attention and respect. Regardless of their different interpretations of the unequivocal sound, the boys knew that the messages were holy and the instructions offered up, if any, had to be heeded to have half a chance that their prayers would be fulfilled. When it came to Rosalinda it was, rather, a quarter of a chance.

The boss, a Dominican, rarely ventured out of the shop, but was aware of these goings on. He did not object, nor did he let the boys know that he knew. On Saturday night, after dinner, he himself would come back to the car wash, with his wife, three young children, and a flashlight. They would kneel in front of the Air Hose with bowed heads. He'd position the tip of his tongue behind his lower teeth, mimicking its sound, and it would hiss back. His wife took a handful of flower petals out of a plastic bag and spread them on the ground around the blessed Air Hose. Then they'd murmur, "Hosanna," repeatedly before returning home, usually hopeful. Sundays the car wash was closed.

alphabetical

when all else fails, when theme and form abandon him, and it feels as though there is no rhyme or reason to fabricate organizing principles, arrange into categories, or impose common meaning where none exists on the pretext of satisfying the vague expectations of academicians or undercover agents intent on extracting the concrete from the intangible and certainty from the obscure, he might as well alphabetize, this being as good an arrangement as any, neither forced nor arbitrary, and yielding an accidental goldmine of its own, giving the inquiring grist for the mill as they suspect a trick and pore over possibilities they are sure are hidden in this strictly ordered yet ambiguous sequence, but should the creator (with a lower case "c" that is) suspect that, in spite of himself, there might be a hidden inadvertent key giving the secret to who knows what away, which would be the last thing he'd choose to do willingly because, who knows, he may well harbor some covert motive he is not fully aware of, well then, he might as well relinquish the alphabetical before starting and pursue instead a course more like the numerical, or nearly so.

And the Winner is .....

She insisted I'd grown worse than I'd ever been, and she really did mean "ever," not merely since she'd known me which was a matter of only a few weeks. I told her she had no basis for making such an assertion about my entire life by relying on evidence to which she had not been privy. I asked her to explain why she stuck with me when she was convinced that I had fallen to such depths. She itemized her purported efforts to rehabilitate me but concluded that none of it worked because of my intractable resistance, although I don't recall her taking any such steps so how could I have resisted? Wasn't it possible, I wanted to know that I was actually better than I have ever been rather than worse? She argued that such a situation would be plausible only if she was less insightful than she'd ever been, which was an impossibility, according to her, because she was born exceedingly insightful and her insight into other people's personalities, emotions, and motives had only grown stronger over the years. The fact of the matter, though, is that I have repeatedly called her insightfulness into question and concluded that it must have diminished greatly from what it had been even before I knew her, that is to say if there was any truth to her claim to being insightful from day one. So, she said, "Well Mr. Smarty Pants, maybe you can tell me how you know so much about my life before we met while you reject my skill in knowing the same about you." Sensing, perhaps, a shadow of hurt on my face, she continued, "Alright, so maybe you're not quite as bad as I made out." Detecting a softening in her stance, perhaps even a cloaked admission of guilt, I started to feel just the slightest bit compassionate myself. Maybe she was, indeed, drawing on some hidden reserves of insight. "Why don't we just call it a draw, Betsy?" "Fine, Richard; you win." "But in a draw," I corrected her, "no one wins."

Andy

the little boy with the wasted leg and the battery operated robot that reached to his knee, set it down on the street in front of his house, where it moved forward and swung its metal arms up and down, and the red plastic bulb of its nose blinked on and off. overcoming its natural unsteadiness and the irregular road surface, it kept going, heading for the middle of the subdivision street where the rush hour traffic had already passed and the school bus had come and gone without the boy because his bad leg was hurting and his mother had said it was alright for him to stay home. he limped after the runaway robot and when it reached the curb across the street, it toppled over and the boy lifted it up and placed it on the neighbor's lawn. the robot had more trouble maneuvering the grass, would go a few inches, fall, and have to be righted. the going was slow, and the boy's leg throbbed from the crouching, so after the robot fell down for the tenth time, the boy let it be, there on its side, without cutting off the power, with the arms and legs still swinging, and the red nose flashing, going nowhere. the boy stretched out on his own side facing the robot that he called Andy (named after himself) and watched its fruitless motion. from their porch, the boy's mother called "Andy, are you alright?" he shut off his robot and shouted back that he was fine, just resting. he grabbed the other Andy and stood up, but his leg buckled, and the two of them were back on the grass, his leg convulsing as he clutched the robot and groaned, "Oh, Andy!" His mother bent down, thrust the robot aside, held him tightly, and cried, "Oh, Andy!"

At the Waterlily Festival

After a good hour of photographing water lilies and lotus, I was drawn to the kids' program at the Reptile Tent by her voice, husky and sweet, explaining the difference between crocodiles and alligators and holding, it seemed, babies of both species. I let the camera dangle from my neck as I wandered over and took a vacant spot on the bench at the end of the second row, joining the crowd of kids and parents. She was holding a baby animal in each hand and talking about their teeth but I was looking at her fearless eyes. I tried to guess, from the few black strands peeking out from under her straw ranger's hat, what her full head of hair was like. She was unconcerned about the alligator nipping at her fingers. She told the kids that crocs preferred salt water while gators go for fresh water. She asked them to make believe they were crocodiles by placing their hands together, finger to finger, rotating them to a horizontal position and lifting them up to their faces to simulate the V-shaped snouts of alligators. Then she had them replicate the U-shaped snouts of crocodiles by keeping that general position but clasping their hands together and interleaving their fingers. The exercise that followed involved exposing their upper and lower teeth like a crocodile, or just their upper teeth like an alligator. The comparisons, for no reason I could fathom, summoned to my mind various differences between water lilies and lotus, how for example the leaves of lilies mostly float upon the water while lotus leaves are propped up above it on sturdy stems. She asked if any kids wanted to volunteer to come on stage and hold an animal. No one did. Neither did the parents, so I raised my hand. "There's a brave man," she said, calling for a round of applause and inviting me up. She handed me a reptile; I don't remember which. The next thing I knew, everything melted away but the two of us. We were in the Florida Everglades on a pontoon, her ranger hat gone and her long black hair billowing gently in the breeze. We were surrounded by baby alligators and crocodiles, the only place in the world where, she said, with its unique combination of fresh and salt water, they lived together. Though carnivores, they happily gobbled up the slices of mango we threw to them, and which we were feeding each other. They escorted us through the lush water habitat in a section of cypress trees and white water lilies. Time seemed both to stand still and be endless as we languidly navigated the Everglades. Eventually, I asked her if she didn't need to get back to finish the show at the Reptile Tent. "Not really," she said, "I never left."

The Bouncing Ball

The green tennis ball would not stop or dare to rest. It was destined to go up and down, high and low, from before to now, and ever after, and woe to anyone interfering. Well versed in man's subversive ways, it evaded the swiping hands seeking to divert or capture it. Continuing to bounce up the street, it found a bus's open door, bounded up the steps, and landed on the gentle driver's head, dribbling as unobtrusively as it could. He thought it was a bird flown in from the open window, and seeing it in the smudged rear view mirror, and certain he detected eyes and a beak, he smiled and patted the tennis ball fondly. "Nice birdy."

But in the back of the bus, the homeless, drug addled militia man raised his erstwhile cane, now a rifle, took aim, and shot. Bull's eye. "Damn pest." It dropped into the bus driver's crotch, a drop of blood staining his pants. In tears, he placed it in his empty metal lunch box, intending to give it a proper burial once he was off his shift. No one else on the bus said a word except the militia man who told the driver to quit his whimpering or he'd be next.

Swiftly, at the next stop, though an open window, a pair of yellow beach balls bounced in and up to the horizontal handrail where they turned into hawks and perched single-mindedly. The militia man must have known what was up for he hit the emergency brake, jolting everyone. He forced the rear door open, but before he could make his getaway, the hawks grabbed him by his camouflage jacket, one to a sleeve, and flew him high above a vast shopping mall. To the horror of the assembled, they released him to meet what everyone was sure would be an unfortunate end.

However, there was neither injury nor splatter and tragedy was averted, for he landed as a basketball, and bounced and bounced along the parking lot, before rolling onto the grassy patch at the traffic light closest to the mall's entrance, the exact spot where he panhandled every morning. There, his old appearance was restored and he began to feel, none too happily, like himself again, flat on his back, hung over and with a splitting headache. A starling on the traffic light knew a charity case when it saw one, and dropped an offering smack onto his face.

Bowing Out

I was nearing the end of my stage career on the streets as each performance took more and more out of me, and I grew winded much more easily. Also, I admitted to myself that I was growing paranoid about the security of my unicycle.

My new unicycle lock was a six foot length of half-inch boron alloy chain hooked to an invincible pick-proof padlock and, with no other place for it, I wore it around my waist as I biked to my venue, a plaza in front of the hotel. The doorman blew his whistle to summon me to the hotel for my scheduled show – alternating acrobatics such as tumbling and torch juggling on foot while my wheel was locked to any sturdy immobile object within sight, with stunts on the cycle.

Working with the concierge and a bel hop, the doorman wriggled me out of the massive chain as I sweated and gasped for breath. I fainted from the stress, just as I imagined they'd be looping the chain through the cycle's wheel as always. However, when I regained consciousness, I found myself locked to a massive tractor by way of a shackle on my ankle, and the key to the lock no longer in my pocket. I'd seen it coming for some time, the doorman's intent to sabotage my performance for his personal gain.

With his wide grin, flamboyant clothing, and sweeping gestures, the consummate performer, he thrilled the audience the way I used to do years ago. The tails of his long red overcoat flapped in the wind as he cycled around the ring in a circus-like environment. With one hand he kept his black top hat from blowing off and with the other he held my whistle. He'd blow it and wink at me each time he completed a circuit. The key to my lock was hanging from his neck.

By this time, quite a crowd had assembled. The children, especially, were enthralled by the doorman's ride, although the parents would be sure to point me out to them as well. They remembered my many performances over the years, perhaps saddened by the knowledge that my best days were behind me. It was heartwarming to see the children's smiles of surprise when they realized I was not a unicycle but a person chained to the tractor which was the star attraction up next.

The doorman's tumbling was somewhat awkward but not all bad, and on the unicycle he was passable as well with the torches though he skipped my signature act of balancing a tureen on my forehead while daintily sipping its lentil soup with a spoon. Perhaps he'd master it one day. Wanting to show him I was not the vindictive type, I tried to toss him a quarter when he held out his upturned hat, but my aim was off and it somehow landed in his barely open mouth. He did not take that very well. He built up speed and stood up on the saddle, doing a little dance in place, while the unicycle coasted around the ring. I tried a jig of my own on the ground, but plopped right back down into the heap of chain. I was applauded for the effort. With difficulty, I got back to my feet to take a bow, but before I could bend, everything started spinning. I fainted again and came to just as the audience was dispersing. I was expecting to be at long last released from my bondage but no one came to my rescue and I was left to rust as week after week the doorman fine-tuned his performance to great acclaim. I did not need the doorman to show me the door, metaphorical albeit. Indeed, I didn't need a door at all, for all the good it would do me. I wish him the best but his time, too, shall come.

Bruno

In the dream, the lady with the rumpled stockings, sunk in the enormous spongy cushion, with her legs spread and her knees reaching her chin, held a small pet rooster by a leash as it pecked around her, and when we asked her where she got this striking specimen of orange and white, she said, "Bruno." "Did you know Bruno?" my wife and I demanded, incredulous that she could have had a tie to our former supervisor when we worked in the aviary. Many thought him deranged but we couldn't have asked for a more understanding boss. He would always cut us slack with our schedules when we needed time off to heal our bodies from the stunts we performed with the birds, and bring us treats from the zoo cafe. And sure enough, yes, that was the Bruno she knew and we reminisced about him and his quirks and how he seemed so overbearing to everyone but the three of us. She didn't divulge her precise relationship with Bruno other than to say he had been exceedingly fond of her and called her, in his softer moments, "my little hen." For sure, not many people got along with him, but we understood he meant no harm by humiliating everyone. It was just his way.

The rooster would periodically venture under the lady's skirts for shelter, it appeared, and pop out again, pecking around that globular and gelatinous cushion which might have been filled with foam, or water, or jello. And all I could think to add was, "Well, I'll be damned. So you knew Bruno?" And she assured us repeatedly that she did and that she had been close to him, extremely close. My wife, though, encouraged me to take a better look at her in her slumped position, and with the winged sunglasses, rhinestone encrusted and crookedly positioned on her face. "She couldn't have known Bruno. Just look at her posture. And those glasses." And it was true Bruno would never have approved of her slovenliness. In her defense, she said that in her younger years her bearing was admired by one and all, Bruno included, and it was only after leaving his employ and falling into hard straits that she began her descent. This we could understand for our own conditions as well had declined upon our separation from Bruno.

The droppings on the ground were making our surroundings increasingly unsightly and my wife had to tiptoe around them in order to get a closer look at the rooster. "What an adorable fowl, a show bird if I ever saw one" she exclaimed. "Oh, yes, he's quite the gentleman," the lady acknowledged. "I call him Bruno." And we agreed that was a fitting name and if he could only somehow be paper trained he would make the perfect pet, and we asked her to keep us in mind if she ever decided to breed him. I asked what it was under her skirts that he found so appealing, but she only smiled modestly, further smudging her already smudged lipstick but, in her favor, also straightening out her sunglasses. Bruno seemed to take this as a hint to make for his sanctuary between her legs, where I lost sight of him. "Well, I'll get to the bottom of this," my wife declared, adamant, and followed Bruno into his roost. With Bruno ensconced with my wife, and the lady beckoning me to come in where it was warm, I couldn't resist. She found the situation amusing and cackled heartily. I could hear Bruno crowing and even my wife tittering. I approached with caution, deciding it might not be so bad a thing for all of us to be conjoined again with Bruno, who always meant us well. A great warm darkness enveloped me as I woke up with a numbness in my wings.

the bundle

a man with a bundle on his shoulder neither big nor small but a bundle, unformed and lumpy, walked towards the stop sign at the intersection. the brown sack could have been filled with rags, or potatoes, or body parts, or everything. the load seemed heavy and awkward though the man did not stoop from the weight. the contents sagged and had to be firmed up every so often. at the stop sign, he stopped. he did not look around to see if he could cross safely. he just stopped and waited, without putting down the bundle. after a while he knelt, but not because of anything resembling tiredness. maybe boredom. maybe he was praying. his eyes were open but looking nowhere. his lips began moving. still kneeling, he was approached by an old woman who briefly glanced at the bundle. he squeezed it tightly and his eyes momentarily took on life as he gave her an angry look. she walked away, quickening her pace. no one else paid him any mind. as dusk came, he took some tools out of a pack he wore around his waist. with these, he took the stop sign off its pole and as it was quite flimsy, he folded it over twice and, looking carefully to be sure he was unobserved, he opened up the bundle and threw it in and returned the tools to their pack. he continued on his way and soon was very small and soon could not be seen any more but the bundle on his shoulder was still visible. when the stars came out, it was still carrying on, far off, moving among them with its own light, determined, looking like it would never stop again.

But Officer

As dusk was approaching, the urban park was rife with white-tailed deer. Slowly and carefully, I drove through the intersection with the four way stop sign. Ahead of me and to the right, a man, knife in his chest and bleeding profusely, ran into the woods. By great and fortunate coincidence, I noticed a police car, sirens and flashing lights at full throttle, on my tail. I pulled over to the side of the road, and the officer stopped behind me.

However, instead of running to aid the victim, he slowly ambled my way, pausing to eye with interest the fawns darting in and out of the bushes but seeming not to notice the marionette dancing on top of the utility pole and whistling at them. Wearing sunglasses and popping gum, the officer fiddled with a computer tablet. Before I could say a word, he asked for my license. A scream came from the woods where the stabbed man had gone.

"But officer, didn't you see the guy with the knife in his chest over there or hear that scream?" "We're not talking about him, bud, but about you. And don't start in about puppets either. I've heard that one before too. License, please." "But you don't understand." "Oh, don't I?" He asked me if I saw the stop sign at the intersection. Now I knew where this was going. He would write me up for doing, what, 1 mile an hour, instead of coming to a complete stop? The usual ploy. Meanwhile, as the sky grew darker, one car after another was zooming through the intersection without so much as slowing down. "Okay, already, I know what you're driving at, but ..." and just then, vanishing into the same dense woods as the injured man, were two teenage boys chasing a woman in a nightgown who was yelling, "Help!"

"Look; look there," I said, alarmed. "No, you look, bud, I'm up to your tricks. I'm no rookie, you know. Don't try to distract me." At that, in the empty playground off to our left, several shady characters were exchanging plastic bags for briefcases. A drug deal was definitely going down. "But officer, there's trouble hereabouts." And losing patience, I said, "Will you get off your butt and take care of these incidents? At least call an ambulance." Before I knew what was happening, he opened my car door, grabbed my arm, dragged me out, and asked me to extend my arms so he could cuff me.

"First your traffic violation, and then insulting a police officer ..... You're in deep doo doo, bud." Looking down at my feet, I saw he was quite correct as I stood in a generous deposit left by one or more deer. Directing my gaze back up I saw he had turned into a buck and, straightaway, bolted. All that was left of his former self was a rumpled uniform. I changed into it, especially welcoming the shiny shoes. The sky was filling with stars. At the intersection, I put up a barricade of flashing lights from his trunk and, through a bullhorn, asked all the approaching cars to line up on the grass, one behind the other. I advised them that the park was closed to vehicular traffic after dark, and that I would be coming by to collect fines, and I didn't want to hear any guff. "But officer ...," they moaned in unison.

Cactus Poacher

He thought he was smart. Nobody was looking and he had his van. It was a big mother, this plant. He was no expert, not about them. Couldn't tell a ferocactus from a furry cactus, but it was a beauty. Three feet around maybe, spiny like hell, red-tipped areoles, looked like it just finished flowering. He grabbed his shovel and made sure the coast was clear. He didn't have to dig very deep or hard, and with a Kevlar suit, padded gloves, and his underwear stuffed with a face towel, he felt invincible. He got the thing up and into his van, chuckling, yipping, and whistling to himself the whole fifty miles home. He stuck it in an old wheelbarrow full of sand, and rolled it into the living room right next to the TV where he could show it off to all his buddies and the occasional ladies he wanted to impress. It wasn't the greatest spot because the light was kind of low, but he wasn't tuned in to things like that. He filled a small juice glass with water, poured it over the top of the cactus to compensate it for the trauma and figured it wouldn't need much water after that, being a desert plant. It looked great, nice and green and threatening. People admired it, especially the ladies, and he told them how he grew it from seed, yep, since he was a kid. In fact, he'd left it with his parents all these years just so they could have some company after he left home and now, them getting old and all, he didn't want them to feel crowded, so he moved it on out to his place. Then one night after the plant had long settled in he struck up a conversation with a tramp named Luette at the Hokey Bar and Grille. He must have seen her leave the place with a dozen guys at least on different occasions. After they each had their third beer and he was going on about his cactus and telling her how it was about to bloom, that it might bloom that very night and that it only blooms for one night a year, well she practically invited herself over. Truth is, the cactus did get five or six puny red buds on it since he lifted it a year ago, but they seemed to him to be starting to shrivel up. He didn't tell that to Luette, of course. He moved the sofa up real close to the cactus and TV and you could tell she was impressed. He didn't waste much time. Got her blouse half open when the crazy cactus actually began to pulse, in and out, like an accordion, first just a little and then a whole lot. She pushed his hands away and her eyes got real wide. She said they had to watch the cactus bloom first and he was pretty bowled over by what was happening. The flowers weren't opening, but little cracks were forming around the plant from the pulsing which turned into a big, heavy heaving, and then it burst, popped all over the place. Hundreds of small brown spiders scurried down the wheelbarrow and towards the couple. One of them jumped into Luette's blouse. She started screaming wildly and yelled for him to help her get the blouse off. But he wasn't up to it anymore and jumped into his van and kept driving till he reached the tropics where he thought he'd try his hand with orchids.

The Carrying Man

The Carrying Man is carrying packages and bundles and loads. With each of his fingers he carries a suitcase or briefcase or garment bag or duffle bag. He balances clothes hampers on his shoulders and oak chests on his nose. Stereo speakers hang from his ears turning cherry red. In his pockets are tenderloin steaks, baked potatoes, boiled cabbage, and French roast coffee. He secures knapsacks, one over the other to his back. Through a belt around his waist he carries nylon mesh shopping bags. Around his ankles are ropes he uses to drag crates filled with insect repellant and other essentials. By crouching slightly as he walks, he can carry cardboard boxes on his knees, or what's left of them. Around his neck dangle numerous purses with heavy coins in twenty five different currencies, just in case he meets up with a foreigner. From his genitals hang a cell phone and laptop, to keep in touch. The Carrying Man is in high form. He is all equipped for a casual walk around the neighborhood. Nothing serious or too far or he may come up short-handed. The Carrying Man keeps his head bare. It helps him think, he says.

Churning Golden

Inside the baby's cry is a gold coin. You can get it by putting another gold coin in the baby's hand. At the mouth of the river, the estuary opens wide to accommodate the pirate ship. The treasure in the baby's voice is golden. Even under the water, bubbles are churning the hearts of sunken pirates. The undercurrent admits no trespassers who have not signed in and paid in gold. The empty pirate ship sways on the little waves like a cradle. Inside the baby's voice are drowned pirates, themselves crying. Their voices are drawn out and smooth, golden and brown like honey sticking to the baby's throat. To lessen the sound, you need to rock the cradle. To soothe the pirates' hearts, you should give them gold. To comfort the spirit of the estuary, you must kiss the baby. Then it will cry with its own voice.

Cluck, Cluck

The old Russian lady, a babushka if I ever saw one, asked me, in broken English, something about chickens, I couldn't quite make out what. Nor could I fathom why she sought me out on this matter but she insisted I had to know since I had authored the definitive encyclopedia, *Shamagandro for Fowl,* But I could only look dumb because I had written no such tract, didn't even understand what the title referred to. Nor could I say I was enlightened when she attempted to set my mind at ease by telling me I was such a kidder and, extending her elbows from her sides, whispered "cluck, cluck." When I laughed, which I couldn't help doing, she poked me in the ribs, telling me that, there, she knew I was just being modest, and, baring her flabby arm, asked if I would autograph her right wing, which I was loathe to touch. She pinched my cheek and pressed me to admit I was the author, even offered to set me up with some good looking pullets, but she was clucking up the wrong tree. She looked incensed and said something about not being one to be trifled with. Ultimately, she shrugged her shoulders and reverted to speaking Russian, which made as much sense as any of it. According to the itinerary she waved in front of my nose, she had a flight departing for Moscow in 3 hours. With

THE SAD PARADE

one hand she picked up her overstuffed shopping bag and with the other a cage with a half dozen chicks. We parted amicably, she for the airport and I to make my evening rounds of the hen house.

Coming Clean

Relaxed and feeling quite weightless, I sit cross-legged, pen and notebook in hand, on a tubular steel frame chair, seat and back of natural cane, and trimmed in maple. Opposite me is an identical unoccupied chair, which I am interviewing, you might say, to get to the root of its problem. This is our tenth counseling session.

"Could you tell me when it started, this *identity conflict*, as you termed it in the questionnaire?" – No answer.

"And your shuddering in our last session, was that an isolated incident or have you experienced it on other occasions?" – No answer.

"I notice your caning starting to fray around the edges. Would you attribute that to standard wear and tear or did you suffer a particular trauma?" – No answer.

I want to ask the chair about the new signs of tarnish but am afraid it will further diminish an already low self-esteem so decide not to probe.

"And pardon my eyesight, but in looking over the medical records from your chiropractor, I can't quite tell whether he wrote that when someone sits on you, it *relieves the sensation* or *relives the sensation*? Nor do I know what sensation is involved. Could you clarify this for me, Mr. Leggett? You don't mind, George, if I call you Mr. Leggett?" – No answer.

"Well, I have good news for you, Mr. Leggett. I see a rather stout and determined looking woman heading straight for you right now. What good fortune. Maybe we'll be able to get to the bottom of things at last. Shall I tell her the chair is free?" – No answer.

The woman barely manages to squeeze onto Mr. Leggett. I hear a stifled moan from underneath her but it could be my imagination. She begins interviewing me.

"So, Mr. Know-it-All, big shot fancy furniture psychoanalyst, what makes you think you are anything other than an empty chair yourself?" Infuriated, I glare at her. "If you'd just look at me," I scream, "you'd have no trouble figuring that out. And why don't you get your prickly behind off my client, you hedgehog." She is silent for a few moments and then writes in her notebook, "No Answer."

The Critical Bite

I finally resolved to ask my dentist whether my exasperated wife's difficulty in extracting information from me about the very ordinary events of my days, which I withheld not out of secretiveness but because there was so little to say was, as she claimed, just like pulling teeth, so there in the chair, I posed my question to him. Scientific to a fault, he wanted to know whether she meant molars, incisors, or what, but I hadn't the faintest, and wasn't about to interrupt his probing in my mouth, to call her then and there to find out because, among other things, she'd probably just scoff at the question, and humiliate me in a voice loud enough for the dentist and his gossipy hygienist to hear. He said he'd help me get to the bottom of her concern, eventually, but for now had to concentrate on my oral cavity. Saying I wouldn't feel a thing, he administered the gas and deep injection, and from somewhere inside my brain I heard the hygienist refer to me as a fool and for an instant I could see them arching over me and kissing. And then the dentist asked whether I was ready for him to begin. When I nodded, he smiled slyly, had me hold the mirror and look inside my mouth, and dangled over my face a forceps gripped tooth, as proof that it was already out. He said he guessed that showed what my wife knew. I agreed wholeheartedly though

THE SAD PARADE

I couldn't quite follow his line of thinking. And when she asked me that night over a dinner of reheated yams and salted mushrooms, her specialty, how the extraction went, I told my wife I could hardly remember, that it was like a dream. It was just like me, she said, to clam up over the slightest question. I long ago gave up trying to profess my innocence, and let her rant, but this time I'd hidden my tooth inside her yam, and was just waiting for her to take the critical bite.

Disappearing

I. Safety Inspection

The Safety Inspector inspected the silver chair I sat in. You were all gold surrounded by the Empress' china. The Safety Inspector didn't like the way I was looking at you. You are intriguing when you undress at the dinner table. I tell the Safety Inspector he can send back the steak if it is not well enough done. You were solid 14K and shook with frenzy on the table while your last piece of underwear fell on the Safety Inspector's plate. Your shaking made me shiver. The Safety Inspector watched your reflection in the Silver Chair but couldn't lift the Empress' tea cup to his lips. The way you held that fork made me want to kiss you wrist. The Safety Inspector placed a hand between his legs and fainted. We shoved him under the table and began our meal.

II. Sleep

She is a spirit who puts people to bed, tucks them in, and so forth. She goes from house to house tucking people in, never reprimanding them for yawning, telling them to sleep well.

She doesn't sleep herself. Each time she must brush back with her hand, her long black hair after bending over drowsy people. She will give you her hand if you reach for it. You yearn so much for her goodnight kiss and struggle fruitlessly to lift your heavy head to meet her but always fall asleep before her lips reach your cheek.

III. Like Smoke

Look into what has melted and the ripple will spread slowly and steadily with the rhythm of abstraction look into what is to come the cup of tea and how empty it is before and after and how it it stares blankly back at you and how when it is filled there will be another look a reflection the tea will steam and you'll inhale the vapor spiraling up from the ripple which you'll swallow as it disappears from the shore of Uruguay where a boy throws stones into the ocean and its impervious water remaining not motionless but still as still as a sprinkler system fanning light jets of water back and forth across a lazy suburban garden.

A Diva's Triumph

The gaunt old man at the recital strained to hear the mezzo soprano's words. His streaming cottony hair and elongated torso understandably annoyed the concertgoers immediately behind him, and his leaning, left, right, and forward, his fidgeting, vexed a wider group. His younger wife, who had given up a promising singing career of her own to marry him, would nudge or pull his shrunken arm to encourage a bit of posture, which he could maintain for 3 minutes at best. His snoring drew more attention to them. The nodding off problem was not new but when they were newlyweds, all she had to do was surreptitiously slide her hand along his inner thigh and he'd wake up alert, anticipating, not always correctly, a post-concert tryst. But lately her efforts only caused him to snore louder. She had lectured him many times at home about how embarrassing his behavior was for her. She threatened to stop going out with him publicly if he persisted in these "antics," as she called them. She reminded him of her aborted stage career and that she still had something of a following. Each time, he vowed to try his best. Of course, she wouldn't reprimand him during an event itself for this would only draw the further ire of their neighbors. Mostly she'd prod and poke him, sometimes exclaiming "Jonathan!" in an exasperated whisper.

But this night he had great trouble controlling his antics. At intermission, she pumped him up with coffee and gave him a good talking to outside the auditorium. She was hopeful that the brisk winter air would keep him awake and steady for the second half of the performance. She hummed to herself the Habanera from Carmen, with which the program was to resume. The mezzo soprano took bows and blew kisses to the appreciative returning audience. But before the pianist could strike a chord, the old man slumped, and dropped down like a log. His wife bent over instinctively and assured herself that he was breathing and had a pulse. Sitting up relieved, not that he was alive, but that he was down, she could almost hear the rest of the audience sigh in equal relief. Soaking in the mezzo's huskily sweet voice, but certain that she herself could have done better, she sat guard, her stockinged foot resting lightly on his chest, making sure he didn't try to get back up. It was an unqualified success. At the program's end, she was sure the ovation was meant as much for her as for anyone.

drinks

it started with breakfast a vile coffee like the dredge of a dredged swamp like the worst nightmares of being lost in the Paris sewers and chased by protoplasmic devils, this sludge next to which Turkish coffee was like spring water had its sequel in the bistro where it was my lot to draw the cup with the broken tea bag and i thought i'd never shake the sensation of slimy leaves snaking down my gullet like hair balls swallowed by the bathtub drain but before i knew it i found myself in a cafe for lunch which didn't have the tonic water i craved so i settled for plain tap water plain except for the insects which swam up to perch on the rim and i wondered if they danced the same dance in my belly and even this revulsion passed as i ran out without paying and bought a container of ice cold orange juice from a street vendor, ran with it to the emptiest street of the emptiest district near the docks but as i put the straw in i hit ice, all ice that would not melt for anything and i cursed at it and threw it in the river, then found a place for dinner but the beer was too weak to take seriously, had a head tasted like dishwater suds and not the slightest kick in creation so i was sure not to try an after dinner drink though the waiter was pushing the Spanish brandy and took offense when i questioned its blue color, well i wasn't about to argue over blue brandy not after this day so when i arrived at Brigitt's apartment near midnight and settled into the rocking chair a parched man i could not believe her offer of port though i'm sure she was well-meaning enough, instead i got raving, swore i'd never touch port, not any port or drinks of any kind and i nodded off rocking and mumbling, would not dream of sipping from Brigitt's breast for fear of gargoyles within, of oceans of unpalatable sour and salty milk, and falling deeper into sleep i saw the Sahara vast and scorched, and how subterranean passages connected it with the Paris sewers, like spider webs of lunacy wet and dry.

The Drunkards and the Meadowlark

He gave the meadowlark a good piece of his mind, the drunkard did, for in his inebriated state, the bird's lovely song was a gross imposition. He raised his slingshot. The fearless bird did not budge but with his aim sorely compromised by the drink, he went far wide of the mark. The rock landed on the left foot of the game warden who hobbled over, none too pleased, and demanded to see the drunkard's permit, which he abashedly proffered. "My good fellow," the warden exclaimed a bit incoherently upon a close examination of the document, "this is only valid for large game – antelope, elk, and the like." He burped for he was something of a tippler himself, and said, "Let the bird be." Not amused, the drunkard pulled a revolver out of his pocket and shot the warden in his already compromised foot. The warden fell and, grabbing his ankle, set about screeching, rather in tune to the meadowlark's melodies. "Now, that duet is music to my ears," announced the drunkard to the warden adding, "Let bygones be bygones." The bullet having gone straight through, the drunkard fashioned a tourniquet from his bandana, wrapped it around the warden's foot, and offered him a nip from his flask. Tears of appreciation fell from the warden's eyes. The two of them began whistling. The meadowlark, still crooning, flew to another perch, ever hopeful for a mate.

Elizabeth

She was a quiet girl, Elizabeth, and a strange girl, her mom thought, for reasons well beyond the obsessive pencil drawings she had made of tree leaves, one to a page, filling sketch pads to capacity. Standing, sitting, kneeling, or lying back on the grassy wooded area along the creek near her home when the weather was balmy, she would draw the leaves hanging from their branches after getting off the school bus one stop early to continue home later on foot. This was her major pastime in the three spring months since her dad's abrupt departure. Her mom praised her work without much studying it. She showed her drawings to no one else. As each of these spiral bound pads was completed, she'd tuck it in a dark corner of the house's crawlspace, under a moth-eaten woolen blanket. One fine day she decided to give up the whole business and went straight home. Her mom was not due home for some hours. She descended to the crawlspace and, with a flashlight, flipped through her drawings, reviewing her handiwork. Unexpectedly, she heard the house door opening and her mom calling from the master bedroom directly above, "Elizabeth." She knew that if she didn't answer, her mom would assume she had gone to the woods to sketch as usual and, desiring that outcome, she remained silent. Her mom called three times, four, followed by quiet, and then her voice again, giggling, and the voice of a man. Elizabeth fluffed up the blanket, turned off the flashlight, and tucked herself in with the hundreds of sketches of leaves. She thought about the book her dad had given her, *The Golden Nature Guide to Trees*, long gone missing, perhaps buried away in some recess of the crawlspace. More intense sounds which she gradually perceived as human came from the bedroom and were joined by a slight rattling of furniture. She tossed off the blanket, curled up in a fetal position and tore leaf after leaf from the pads, letting them settle around her, until there was nothing left.

Escapades at the Beach

In the Ladies' Changing Room, the conversation of Ladies A and B centered around Lady B, whom Lady A said (addressing her simply as B) was, in essence disrobing earlier in the morning when she removed the belt from her dress as the two of them strolled together back and forth the length of the very long boardwalk, a morning routine that preceded lunch and their afternoon swim. The other women in the changing room, in their various states of dress and undress, pretended to ignore the banter, but their ears were glued to every word, as Ladies A and B slowly changed into their swimsuits.

Lady B denied that it could in any sense be construed as disrobing for it was a brutally hot day, hotter than either of them had anticipated and, had she known, she would not have worn the belt in the first place. Lady B said that it pinched her and made her waist sweaty. She further denied Lady A's accusations of exhibitionism. Lady B reminded Lady A that she had at first simply loosened the belt, but within a few minutes realized that this measure was insufficient to provide the relief she needed, so she unbuckled it entirely, thinking to herself "Oh, what the hell, so what?"

The action of undoing the belt, a series of interlinked steel and leather rings, was to Lady A no less than what she now referred to as "whipping it off". Did she not realize, Lady A wanted to know, that everyone's heads turned from the waterfront to Lady B's waist, and that if she was not embarrassed for herself, Lady B ought to have been for Lady A, her nearest and dearest friend. And it is a fact, Lady A continued, that the people, the men in particular, though not exclusively, began to examine the rest of Lady B's physiognomy, albeit modestly attired, above and below the waist.

It was clear, said Lady A, that they wanted that belt for their own diversion, as a keepsake or fetish, this due in no small part to the way Lady B displayed it. Lady A said Lady B let it dangle from her hand, sending a signal to her admirers that she wanted nothing better than for them to vie for the prize. The winner would get to keep the belt, perhaps even Lady B. Lady B dismissed as nonsense the insinuation that she was suggestively displaying the belt in the hopes of attracting no less than a replacement for Lady A.

And so their discussion continued in the changing room for the time it took them to wiggle into their very brief bikinis. As Lady B was about to put her clothes in their joint locker, she realized that her belt was nowhere in sight. The both of them searched for it to no avail. Lady A said it served Lady B right, for acting so childishly provocative, but she was willing to drop the whole issue as long as Lady B would not repeat a scene of that nature. That was fine with Lady B, although she did not know precisely what "a scene of that nature" entailed.

After frolicking in the water, they retired to their private cove, a spot typically ignored by the rest of the beachgoers, where they had taken many pleasurable hours, and were surprised to come upon a seated group of men and women in a circle. They couldn't tell at first, but Ladies A and B soon realized these people were nude and they were passing, from one to the next, like a peace pipe, Lady B's belt, smelling it, stroking it. They welcomed Ladies A and B and were quite excited at the prospect of perhaps passing Lady B and even her fussy companion, Lady A around, as well. It did not take much for the group to induce Lady A to return to the locker and retrieve her own belt as well for the mutual consolation of all involved. No sense being argumentative or resistant at this juncture, so everyone got very cozy and Ladies A and B resolved to bury, if not the belts, at least the hatchet.

Exhausted

I had exhausted all the other possibilities and grew weary of falling for the temptations that did not deliver, which is why I made my way back to Khan al-Khalili, to sit on a stubby legged stool in a cafe with other old men, smoking a shisha and trying hard not to reflect.

I had been the recipient of too many *no's* and was tired of sifting through mostly insincere and unreliable *maybes* for the distant prospect of a *yes*, provided life was long enough, and it was not a *yes* with conditions or clauses or small print that I sought, or one that might be a *no* in disguise.

Given my suspect condition, bleary eyed and scraggly bearded, with sloppily forged documents, there weren't many other places I'd be taken in, no questions asked. Thus, my return to Khan al-Khalili. Here, I didn't have to exert myself and wasn't plagued by doubt. All I got were lies, pure and simple. It was a relief not to be guessing. I could just sit and smoke. That, and be left alone. Maybe some backgammon, chess, or dominoes if I felt sociable. And if I wanted an excursion, I had the bazaar, steps away, street after winding street of brass and silk, perfume and oils, baskets and lanterns and lights, and colors to shame the imagination.

I knew this too would become tiresome, and I'd revert to harboring new expectations. I'd struggle to catch my breath and hardly knew what from. It's happened before, and is always in the cards. I relinquish the sanctuary, venture outside the quarter, scrutinize faces, and wonder, "Will this one say *yes*, that one?" My disappointment is a foregone conclusion. After a while I just might shave, to prepare for my inevitable return back, yet again, in a new guise, to Khan al-Khalili and, this time, pretend I'm somebody I don't know, which is not so far from the truth.

Fair Trade

There on the bench of the bus kiosk, it looked like he was petting or cradling a small pet, maybe a rabbit but, getting closer, I saw he was only manipulating his wallet, arranging credit cards, photos, paper money, lots of it. I wanted to go up to him and slap that wallet out of his hands and order him not to dare pick it up, and in its place, to give him anything living - a guinea pig, say, mottled black and brown on white, that he could grow to love, but I had no such pet at hand. I didn't want the moment of opportunity to slip by so I took off one of my woolen gloves and told him that from here on in, this would be Fred, his new companion, and I demanded that he show it some affection right away. The need in him was apparently intuitive and intense for he set to stroking it without delay, having some difficulty deciding, though, which side was up. I backed away slowly and more and more he looked to me like he could have been someone just searching through his wallet. But this was no longer the case. He was bringing a love to life. Meanwhile, I was suddenly the proud recipient of a new identity and rather well to do.

A Family Tale

"Mom, look I've got a tail." "Look, Roger, he's got a tail." But Roger wouldn't look anymore. He'd seen enough, told her their son was going too far, wiggling his behind around, in the street yet, pretending to be some kind of canine. The excursion to the neighborhood picnic was turning out to be anything but pleasant. "But isn't he cute, Roger?" He told her the behavior was anything but, and that she should tell the boy to quit fantasizing, before he took his belt to him. It was time he grew up. Billy started sobbing, and quit wagging his behind. "Look what you've done, Roger. Has your tail gone limp, Billy?" In tears, he nodded. Roger told her it was about time she and the kid faced up to reality, but she wouldn't relent. "Tell him he's got a tail. Tell him you believe. What's it to you?" And she set about crying herself. Roger quickened his pace to distance himself from them. "It's a beautiful tail," she whispered to Billy, and he perked up, and started wiggling again. Roger was a full block ahead of them, and didn't look back. She and Billy hailed a taxi. They'd skip the picnic and take refuge at her mother's. "Kid and his damn tail," he grumbled, as they passed him in the taxi. "She's no better than him, the slut, the way she jiggles that rear of hers around. How'd they like it if I cut his stupid thing off, hers too for that matter, and just let them bleed until they dropped. See what the bitch says then." Old Mrs. Tagel served her daughter and Billy hot chocolate and listened, incensed, to the story. In the attic, stooped over, she scrounged around for just the right doll. She carefully pulled three pins from out of her apron's hem and stuck them into the doll's lower back. At that very moment, Roger, passing through a subway turnstile, on the way to a bar where he could take comfort felt a fierce itching at the base of his spine.

The Firewood

The matter at hand was removing the firewood, and since the pile sat on their common property line, the question arose of who would be responsible, Mr. A or Mr. B. Mr. A was the one who wanted it done so he could erect a wrought iron fence, but the wood belonged to Mr. B, who stockpiled it years ago, after he moved into the house. Mr. B discovered, though, that fireplaces were too much trouble, so the firewood languished, and this was a good opportunity to have the wood hauled off. Being amiable neighbors, their first idea was to do it together, an unrealistic and ill-conceived idea, for Mr. A was old and infirm and the younger Mr. B claimed to "suffer," (and he'd always emphasize that verb) from a bad back. Thus, they more sensibly resolved to have somebody else do the job.

Mr. A said, "You know, of course, my son is in that line of business, I mean to say hauling, but he'd never take money from me or from a neighbor." Mr. B said, "Well all you can do is ask. I wouldn't want him doing it for nothing." So Mr. A asked his son, Junior A1, who said no, he would never take money from his father or any neighbor of his father's. But regardless, he was too tied up to do the work right then. He

THE SAD PARADE

offered to speak to his brother, Junior A2, who worked for a competitor's hauling company, but with whom the father, Mr. A had broken all relations.

"Over my dead body," said Mr. A. Junior A1 replied, "Alright, if that's how you want it, but you'll have to wait until I can fit it in, Dad, and you know when the time comes, I won't take any money." Well Mr. A was in a bit of a rush to get the fence up and acceded to having his estranged son, Junior A2 put it up, as long as the father could be absent from the negotiations, for surely Junior A2 would expect to be paid, and handsomely. It was arranged that Mr. A would pass payment to Junior A2 through Junior A1.

Mr. A communicated to Mr. B that the work would be done, and that they would share the expenses. Mr. B was pleased to hear about this apparent softening in Junior A1's attitude towards accepting payment or at least serving as a funnel for it. But when Mr. A went on to relate that the work itself would be done by Junior A2, Mr. B unexpectedly soured on the project. "As I recall," he said to Mr. A, "doesn't Junior A2 have a criminal record? I'm not sure I want him digging around my property. Who knows what he'll bury." The coarseness of Mr. B's language escalated as he continued to vilify Junior A2.

Well, Mr. A got plenty upset at Mr. B for talking like that, and answered, "I know he's a good for nothing, but you've got no call to be talking about him that way. I would hope you'd respect that, low-life scum that he is, he's my son. I didn't want to wait forever to get my iron fence up, so I figured I could put up with some personal discomfort by having that jackass do the work. Why don't you go ahead and move the firewood yourself. You're young and strong. And don't give me that malarkey about your back. I've seen you working plenty hard in your yard. Back trouble, my back end!"

These words from his good neighbor got Mr. B angrier than he had ever been about just anything. That Mr. A had somehow seen through his tried and true excuse for avoiding almost anything - his back - was a sharp blow to Mr. B's confidence in his skill at deception. It got him so angry, in fact, that he murdered Mr. A, bludgeoned him with a spade, then looked up Junior A2, the bad son, whom he had spoken against bitterly. Junior A2 was glad to hear the news about his father's demise, and arranged it so that his pop was chopped up and put into several of the larger firewood logs, which the son hollowed out himself. He plugged the ends up properly with wood chips and glue. The spade he promised to send up in smoke in his foundry's furnace. The whole job cost Mr. B plenty, not the least of which was dealing with Junior A2, but it was worth it.

A few days later, Junior A1 realized that his father had disappeared. He notified Junior A2 of this troubling fact. Junior A2 told his brother not to worry. Regrettably, he said, their father had eloped to some unknown destination with a gold digger. Junior A2 went on to lie that the only reason he knew about this was because the gold digger in question had been in the employ of Junior A2. This rashness of the father angered Junior A1, the good son, who said to his brother, "I wash my hands of him for good. I guess you were right all along."

With an unexpected lull in Junior A1's schedule, he decided, despite his newfound hatred for his father to honor the commitment to have the firewood, his father's remains included therein, hauled to the wood bank. He also decided to undertake the work himself, and forego any payment. He would thus spare Mr. B from having to pay Junior A2 the entire cost, in the eloped father's absence. This suited Junior A2 very well also. "That will be an end of it," they both thought to themselves for very different reasons.

"That will be an end of it," refrained Mr. B. He was especially glad to be rid of the firewood, fence or no fence. He did feel some slight tinge of remorse, but not enough to keep him from calling the police and implicating the brothers A1 and A2 in the crime concerning their father, who had met a most tragic end, as Mr. B put it. He had seen the murder, the mutilation, the whole horrible thing. Unfortunately, his bad back kept him from preventing it or calling the police until now.

"This will surely wrap things up," thought Mr. B in his rocking chair, awaiting the police visit, at the same time as Junior A2 was rocking in his own, twirling the still unincinerated spade in his hand, and wondering to what additional profitable use he might put it.

For the Erasing of Difficulties

The formula is long vanished. It cured "pain" or "suffering," as variously translated. Some said it was a cream to rub on the chest, over the heart. Others claimed it was an elixir, to be mixed, just before drinking, with an elderberry wine infused with secret herbs. One smudged manuscript suggested it was a prayer to be whispered in Greek. A moth-eaten Chinese scroll described it as a hymn to be sung from atop a certain coastal rock outcropping. Precise details were always lacking. The chieftain of a modern-day nomadic tribe living in a remote wilderness, cited in a reference to the formula etched on an elk antler, was asked by an anthropologist whether he had ever heard of an ancient formula for the erasing of difficulties. He rubbed his chin and shook his head somberly, before breaking out into a rollicking laugh as though making a mockery of the question. In this he was joined by every last member of the tribe, the ill and infirm included, nor were the wild animals exempt, and it resounded throughout the hills.

For the Greater Good

On a bright April morning, heading toward the lake with the other early risers, like programmed zombies, I notice in front of me an angler with an odd gait. I realize it is not a fishing rod he is carrying but a decorative metal curtain rod. I tap him on the shoulder and say, "Won't catch much with that, pal." He turns around and I see that he is a merman, scaly and otherwise fish like below the waist. He smiles, raises the rod as if in a sign of welcome, and brings it down viciously upon my head. When I come to, I am naked, tied to a spit, and starting to seriously feel the heat. His mermaid wife is sprinkling me with coarse salt. "Kosher?" I ask, just before she stuffs a small apple into my mouth. I observe that she has more hungry mouths to feed when her young offspring cautiously venture out from behind her massive anal fin. At the sight of me being basted in my own perspiration, they excitedly flip their tails side to side, at the same time sweeping paprika from the ground onto my reddening torso. Even if the apple weren't occupying every last corner of my oral cavity, how could I in good conscience plead for mercy and deprive this family of a decent meal? So, as the flames singe my hair, I hum a few bars of Auld Lang Syne and give myself up to the moment.

General Kigoshi Fujiwara's Dilemma

His troops by the thousands were massed all around him, primed with their rifles and telescopes raised high, intent on the devious enemy, and awaiting the signal from the General, a clang from his monumental bronze temple bell. His instincts told him to attack without delay. Waiting, even seconds more, would allow his foe to take flight, to escape into thin air. And nothing was holding him back except the awful mosquito bite on his right cheek. The one armed general, firmly gripping the chestnut mallet in his right hand, knew that the only way he could relieve his itch was to drop it and scratch and oh, how tempted he was to do just that but for the call to a higher duty and the eyes of all the helmeted soldiers upon him, ready to serve their leader to the death. He had never succumbed to prevarication nor would he this time. To think that a nasty mosquito might unseat the established order, re-draw national borders, and indeed disrupt the foretold course of history seemed absurd and he would not let it happen. So, steeling himself to the awful bite, swallowing the pain because the infernal itch was as penetrating, deep seated and persistent as any of the battle wounds he had suffered, he drew back his overcompensating muscular right arm and swept it forward in a mighty horizontal arc so the mallet struck the bell of his ancestors with the mightiest of clangs that surely the whole kingdom if not the heavens themselves could hear. At that the soldiers took their final split second aim and fired, as planned, at the barely visible mosquito hovering just inches above the General's head, with a display of firepower never before unleashed by these matchless forces. And with that, they tossed their arms down and their helmets into the air in celebration, certain that their target was demolished and not even bothering to look for its remains as it deserved anything but a proper burial. The General, meanwhile, set aside his mallet and scratched his cheek with unending sighs and moans of pleasure. Nurses rushed up to him with cold compresses and salves to alleviate the irritation. Cheers pulsed through the troops and beer was consumed in prodigious quantities. A makeshift platform was constructed among calls for a speech. Silence descended upon the crowd as the General mounted the platform. No sooner did he raise his solitary arm in triumph and begin, "My friends …," than he heard millimeters from his left cheek, as did everyone else through the loudspeakers, an angry buzzing, and feel the sharp sting of a familiar proboscis penetrating his flesh. Furious, he drew his sword, waving it through the air on every side of himself, high and low, as if battling an invisible enemy. Ultimately, realizing the futility of it all and plagued by what were now two itching cheeks and the swarms of his men watching aghast, he saluted the victorious mosquito with the hilt of his sword. No sooner done, he resolved to undergo a ritual to which he had never expected to resort - he turned the blade upon himself and thrust, settling the matter once and for all, and honorably.

Getting There

At the airport car rental office, asking directions to the Hyatt, I hear from a clerk whose name tag says Harry, "Well, I'm not really sure the best way - I don't go downtown much. Do you know, Harriet?" and Harriet says "We stayed at the Hyatt for our honeymoon but God knows how Herman got there. We were stoned out of our minds anyway."

Eventually they get the manager, Mr. Henry, involved, and 3 people are conferring over a map and drawing lines and arrows in red, which are obliterating street names, and giving me their own versions of the best way to the Hyatt, and are on the verge of reaching a consensus, when Harriet notes, "Hey, its rush hour. He can't use I-70. It'll take him forever." Harry's and Mr. Henry's faces assume unique expressions of revelation. They shake their heads in agreement, and Harry says, "You know Harriet is right - I-70 would be quicksand."

So, it's back to the drawing board and eventually they come to a new conclusion, this time drawing over the same map with green ink, trying to make it easier for me to see, and I am furiously taking down their verbal directions on what is left of the napkin that came with the honey roasted peanuts on my flight in. With other customers impatiently waiting while I am catered to by the entire staff, things get harried and confused. Harriet is going off duty but is sure I'll be in good hands with the others. She assures me they'll get me to my hotel just fine, and even if I get lost, she says, it'll be no great loss, for the Hyatt isn't living up to its standards of days gone by.

Grabbing the red and green over-scribbled map and my peanut napkin, I notice, on the way to the exit, a computerized system of accommodation addresses and directions, called the "Happy Hotel Hunter." I follow the menus on the touch screen and get a printout with yet another route to the Hyatt, which I hope to reconcile with my map and written directions. At the bottom of the printout is a fortune cookie like message - "The reward of long looking is happy finding." I miraculously locate the hotel, except it seems my reservation was not at the Downtown Hyatt at all, but at the Airport Hyatt, for which I didn't need a car in the first place.

I drive back to the airport, return the car, and walk to the Airport Hyatt, where they determine that what I really want is the Hyatt at the airport across town. I get the rental car again, and go through another ordeal of directions and maps. This time, the computer generated route comforts me with the saying, "Be patient and you will get there." I arrive at the other Airport Hyatt after midnight. There they tell me that they were only able to hold my room till 10 PM, since I didn't leave a credit card number, and with the big aviation convention, rooms were in great demand. They are willing to check the downtown Hyatt for vacancies.

I tell them not to bother, that I am too worn out, and begin to suspect that I may have landed in the wrong city. I go back to the first airport and decide to sleep in its enormous parking lot, in the rental car, under the roaring jets. I seem to see Harry and Harriet and Mr. Henry, waving from the van next to me, but I'm too sleepy to check if my eyes are playing a trick. The van is gone the next morning, when I catch a flight home, not sure why I ever came, but convinced that I didn't miss anything.

Going Up

Breakfast buffet in yet another convention hotel lobby ballroom where I am awaiting the start of yet another convention, this one on the Global Elevator Industry. I avoid people I know, and sit at a narrow counter facing a wall with posters advertising a new line of Chinese super speed elevators they are touting as "supersonic," a mis-translation I suppose. Next to me a man says to a woman, "I came down too hard, too fast." Long ago, I gave up trying to make sense of conversational fragments but given the nature of the meeting it seemed rather obvious what he was referring to. I was curious but did not want to intrude on their tête-à-tête and, besides, realized I forgot my name badge, and had to head back up to my room.

The elevator, a French Smooth Wizard Model 151K skips my floor, 5, and goes straight up to 25, the top floor, where the doors open and it's twilight already. "Time flies in the Smooth Wizard," their slogan, I remember from my training days. I press 5 but the doors won't close. Next elevator down, the loudspeaker tells me, is not until midnight. "What? You must be crazy. Where's the manager?" I ask the disembodied voice which is actually listening. I'm not concerned that I will miss, already have, in fact, the day's talks but I don't want to be stuck on 25 for 4 more hours. Miss Dupré, the manager, is occupied," the voice answers, "dusting porcelain busts of Napoleon in the Executive Suite on 25," as if I cared.

The doors to the two stairwells on 25 seem to be locked. I find the Executive Suite and knock loudly and often but either Miss Dupré has finished her work and is no longer there, or she doesn't hear me or doesn't choose to answer. I take a seat in the hallways next to the door, on a Louis XIV armchair upholstered in gold stripes and grip tightly the elegantly curved arms, imagining a massive elevator filled with just such chairs. On the other side of me is an open window. I contemplate, though not seriously, scaling the building down to my floor. A waitress in a skimpy costume approaches, offering me cocktails, which I decline. "Stuck?" she asks, and pulls, from her cleavage, a key on a string hanging from a leather collar constricting her smooth white neck. The antique brass key is marked VIP, the same letters etched on the private elevator adjacent to the other side of the Executive Suite. I try the key, and it fits. I enter. The door closes. The elevator is ancient and rickety, but functional. I press 5, the only floor for which there is a button and it starts moving but up, I soon realize, rather than down. I am still going up.

His Trembling Left Hand

It arose spontaneously one morning, and ever after came and went of its own volition. Its fluttering was magnified by the composure of the rest of his body. Once it took its course, there was no stopping it, until it had enough. In company, he would exercise temporary control by pressing it against his body or squeezing it with his other hand, but one could easily see that this was a halfway measure at best. Everyone pretended not to notice but no one fooled him. He also used to clasp his hands behind his back once it started, but gave this up because he grew to feel there was something dishonest about total concealment, and thought it engendered more than average pity in onlookers. People took their guesses, foremost being Parkinson's and other neurological disorders, but he admitted to nothing, and never had his condition medically examined. He was free of other symptoms. Although he was grateful only one hand was affected, it somehow upset his sense of symmetry.

He would dream, all evidence to the contrary, that one morning he would wake up and the trembling would be gone but, invariably, turbulent mini-waves arose in his first cup of coffee, which clattered as he set it down. He learned just how much coffee he could pour to avoid spills. Tulip shaped wineglasses filled one quarter to one third full required no adjustments. Sometimes, when alone and unoccupied, he would lay his hand, palm up, on a table or desk and incredulously watch the incessant movement, especially of his fingers, and be reminded of a horshoe crab. He tried mind control, without success, to will it to stop. When his hand was in its off mode, he would exuberantly seek out people, those he knew and strangers, to show them he was fine, as normal as the next man. But it wouldn't last. The duration of oscillations and the intervals between them were unpredictable, as was the timing of their onset.

One day in a supermarket he noticed a beautiful woman selecting peaches but was too self-conscious about his hand, inactive at that moment, to approach her, so he went his own way up and down the aisles. Later, he found himself behind her in the checkout line. Their eyes met. He felt sure she'd be compassionate enough not to let a wayward hand derail a relationship. He couldn't believe his eyes, though, watching her try to swipe her credit card with a trembling right hand. Like the contagiousness of a yawn, his left hand, setting a bag of peaches on the belt, followed suit. She was transfixed by his hand but, soon, fear swept across her face. He abandoned his shopping cart and bolted to the parking lot. In the back seat of his car, he assumed a fetal position, his left hand between his thighs, squeezing it as hard as he could bear. His whole body convulsing, he released a long accumulated stream of tears.

Hot Goods

There he was, the policeman, Officer Patrick, in full uniform, badge and all, with two masked accomplices, stealthily sliding the Viking Eight Burner Range to the loading dock of Delaney's Professional Appliance Land where I was the night watchman. I knew Officer Patrick well, often playing against him in our monthly pinochle tournaments at the precinct after hours. I used to wonder about the way he shuffled the deck but never took him for a thief. "Ah, Romero," he said, "I'm so glad to see you; we could use a hand." "But Officer Patrick, how will I ever explain this to Mr. Delaney? "You've got your imagination. Now come on." I helped them maneuver it through the massive sliding doors and onto a waiting fire truck, presumably stolen as well. There were 3 gagged firemen, hands behind their backs and tied to their ankles quivering in a corner of the truck. "Nice job, Romero" he complimented me. And then whispered in my ear, "I'll be back tomorrow night, alone. I've had my eye on that Lynx infrared grill; what a beauty!" I stood in the loading dock, fearful for my job and worse repercussions. Officer Patrick waved goodbye to me and shouted to someone inside, "Okay, Boys, ready to roll," and as I heard the engine start, I saw the driver, Mr. Delaney puffing away with glee on his big cigar and high fiving Officer Patrick. And off they went burning rubber and who knows what else.

In my Impossible Dream

I am not Don Quixote, but a radish, running a 400-meter sprint, taking the lead as soon as the pistol is fired and not giving it up but blacking out as I am just about to reach the finish line and, Sisyphus-like, starting the race again. It may be impossible for me to ever finish but not unreasonable, it strikes me, because I can, at least, imagine victory.

In my condition, though, which is to say as a radish, stuck here in the earth, incapable of taking even a step, what are my real world chances? I wouldn't refuse an assist from a good Samaritan who might pluck me from the ground, trim my roots, snap off my greens and, thus, pared down to my aerodynamic best, give me a head start, and roll me down the track with a big heave ho. What would prevent me from sprouting legs and a body streamlined and energized for racing?

I've always said that all it takes is getting a little shove in the right direction for the inconceivable to make sense and, if this is wishful thinking, which I am prone to, I admit, let me aim instead for a more relaxed relay event. Good team mates, a turnip, carrot, and kohlrabi, perhaps, could make all the difference. Surely we deserve more than to be salad ingredients. Deliver us from the grater and we will deliver victory.

Jowls

I was sure I saw George Washington's jowls staring at me from a collage of auto parts on the wall of the junk shop but when I looked very carefully, it was a pair of ordinary jowls, not those of the father of our country and certainly not those of the boy who cut down the cherry tree since the ones I was looking at were flaccid and aged and absolutely nondescript, could not have belonged to anyone who would ever amount to anything or had any greatness in his life, yet they did remind me, the more I looked, of the tango drummer, Don Felipe, in Buenos Aires, who grew only more accomplished with age, and how his jowls would flap as he hit the drums, how like they were to the small breasts of those elderly African tribeswomen who danced to the drumbeats of their men, the men who sang so much, their taut facial muscles allowed of no jowls whatsoever, so they would widen their cheeks and jaws, with disks of wood and each of them would take into battle the name of George, and they would be brave, crossing the Delaware, the Nile, the lot of them.

Ken Who?

a person is calling me, trying to call me, trying to reach me. others take the message, because i am often out of my office, at meetings or on travel. they continue to take the message, or messages of the person, which is that he called. i do not recognize the name, Ken Gabber, was it? that is all he leaves, that, and that he's calling from Chicago. but he doesn't leave a number for me to return the call, and he doesn't say whether he'll call back, but he does, over and again, and only when I'm away. my colleagues and the secretary say this Ken Gabber is sure trying hard to reach me, must be something important, and all i think is that it's nobody i know or need to know or want to know. Ken who? did she say. Gabber? Grabber? strange name. could be someone soliciting who got my business number. could be someone mistakenly referred to me when the matter could have been handled by a low level clerk just as well. could be anything, maybe something important after all, i decide, so i cut down on my time away from the office, pare back my travel schedule, make excuses for not attending meetings, and still i seem to just miss Ken, who keeps calling, but when i'm not there. eventually i do not leave my office, forego important outside meetings and activities that would take me away, jeopardize my job in the process, eat lunch at my desk, eliminate breaks, go to the bathroom only when absolutely necessary, and even take to spending my evenings and weekends there. i tell everybody, the secretary included, to let me take all the calls, on the chance it could be Ken, on the chance we'd get disconnected if someone tried to transfer the call. i neglect all my other work. my hand is on the phone at all times. i barely wait for it to ring and, as soon as it does, I flick the receiver to my ear. i don't give the person a chance to speak. i shout into the phone, "Ken, is it you? is it you, Ken? are you Ken from Chicago? who are you, Ken?"

The Key Thing

Finally, after a good week wandering the desert, I stumbled upon a movie theatre style popcorn machine among a stand of sagebrush. It advertised, "Keys Made in One Minute or Less. Free today. Insert key here," with an arrow pointing to a slot on the side. The padlocked shackles around the ankles of my bare feet were wearing me down and I was sick and tired of hopping about. I knew that the key I was holding didn't fit the padlock. I remembered, though, that I was on a mission to make copies. I dropped it into the machine. A few lizards and snakes stopped to watch the puffed-up kernels smashing against the glass sides of the popper as the clanking sounds of the key being duplicated took place out of sight. In 46 seconds, by my watch, a recorded robotic voice announced, "Keys ready." I pushed open the hinged plastic door to a receptacle just under the slot to find my original and duplicate on a ring next to a small bag of popcorn. My feet were bruised and swollen from the shackles but I was able to make it to the hotel which materialized out of the haze - Larry's Honeymoon Suites.

At the desk, a frowning clerk in a grey pill box hat with "Larry" engraved on his brass name badge asked me for a form of ID.

THE SAD PARADE

Trying my best to be unobtrusive, I slipped the bag of popcorn into his open palm. "Will this do, Larry?" He immediately stashed it in the small safe on the desk and slammed the door closed, giving the combination lock a few brisk spins. He asked whether I ever found the key to Maggie's room. I slammed the ring of two keys onto the desk. Once he thoroughly examined them, his disapproving expression vanished. He smiled, shook my hand, and greeted me. "Welcome back, you old devil. Give 'em here." He dangled them from the end of a thick wooden dowel on which a parrot perched. "No need to lock rooms in the Honeymoon Suites as you well know. I expect you'll want your usual. She's still in Room 300. No doubt you'll have no trouble finding your way. I'll go ahead and ring up." I took the elevator to 3. I was about to knock when a man in sorry looking shackled feet like my own hopped out the door and down the stairs. "Sweetheart!" I was greeted by a half-dressed woman starting to look familiar, "Did you remember to bring your Maggie that popcorn?" She coyly pretended to hide a hefty pair of compound bolt cutters behind her back. "But I, I thought Larry ...," I stammered before fainting.

When I came to, I was in a locked metal cage that I couldn't stand up in. Just outside the cage playing on a TV there was a short continuous loop video of Maggie in a bikini, dancing suggestively with the bolt cutters. Now and then, she'd bend down to let Larry, whose legs and torso were bound to a chair, feed her popcorn. Off to the side was the safe, open and empty. On top, the parrot jiggled the keys when the spirit struck. I am still holding out hope.

The Last Attack upon the Wiggly Man

We can get him now, the Wiggly Man. We can get him and straighten him up, iron him out, plaster him, that wriggly Wiggly Man. We can put him in cardboard and giftwrap him, that squiggly man. And he'll no longer saunter off in the middle of the night to wriggle on the ground and up buildings, no longer swim through your plumbing system and wind up in your kitchen sink in the morning. This will be the last attack and this is how we'll do it. We'll lure him into a trap with a curvy, swervy woman. A nervy woman unintimidated by the squiggly man. She will draw him into her lair and offer to jiggle and flatten herself upon her bed for him but will, instead, ply him with drink, take him unawares and flatten him cold upon her wild tiled bathroom floor with her rubbery pink parasol. This will be the demise of the Wiggly Man – until one Christmas morning – a husband and wife present their snuggly, cuddly half-asleep daughter with a gift they found languishing in the corner of a musty, dusty thrift store. Unwrapping him to her delight and that of her parents, all three uncontrollably giggling, she wiggles him back out of shape and into his old irredeemable squiggly self.

Midge's Fortunate Detour

When Midge turned 16, her wheelchair turned 1. A person grows accustomed. She had no complaints, only aspirations. She did everything a 16-year-old girl in a wheelchair could be expected to do, unfailingly rolling (weather permitting, each morning,) down and back the level mile long path along the creek near her home, rather fed up with her parents' incessant admonitions to "be careful" spoken almost in unison, and over her repeated objections. In fact, it was on her birthday that she got up early enough, 5 AM, while her parents were still asleep, to roll out the door and avoid what would have surely been an over the top fuss. She followed from a distance what looked like a fox slithering toward the creek but a small dip in the ground threw her off course and she got caught in some thorny bushes, preventing her from backing up or continuing forward. At least she was in view of the path. She didn't want to shout for help indiscriminately so patiently waited for a pedestrian to come into view. Eventually she saw a partially obscured bicyclist and shouted to him, "Excuse me." He approached. He turned out to be a young man, about her own age, not on a bike after all but also in a wheelchair, smiling, telling her not to worry. She cautioned him not to approach or he'd get stuck as well but he continued toward her. Their two left wheels gently bumped into each other. They rattled for a second and she could see he had become trapped too. "I'm so sorry," she cried. He smiled, told her not to worry and pulled a pair of garden pruners from a leather holster looped onto an arm of his wheelchair. "Happened to me once," he said, "and I got scratched up pretty bad getting out so I always carry these." Each looked upon the other's eyes as if they were pools of memory and anticipation. "I'm Jordan." "Midge," she said. With a few well targeted clips, he had them gallantly extracted from the vegetation. They rolled back up to the path together, side by side, disentangled and forever inseparable.

Nothing to Speak Of

The times in the immeasurable past when I spoke endlessly of everything I or anyone could imagine not a topic I would leave unturned untouched and it would be with my whole body not just the lips and I spoke flesh and blood not just words and all heedlessly headlong by intention always striking the mark my pronouncements awaited with great expectation lauded and applauded in the furthest recesses of this and every universe.

All ears turned my way alert attentive taking in each and every message sent forth in every direction but with time though I continued to project well enough and my voice remained clear the force the volume diminished and I would supplement with my hands drawing figures in the air my body gesticulating my eyes alight through it all my spirit undiminished or so I thought the news I was so determined to deliver still broadcast and I hoped worth hearing.

After a time I was delivering fewer words with less enthusiasm and receiving I had to admit not the robust accolades to which I had grown accustomed but still I was convinced I had heart and conviction which should count for plenty and still there were the faithful followers and ears fewer perhaps turned to my speech but now and then I had no doubt they gathered a snippet if no more of what I was making a case for and they must have understood at least now and again and could repeat it back to me with their own voices had I the nerve to ask so that I felt I was not totally without influence or abandoned it could not be all bad if I needed my hands and toes to count their numbers or perhaps just my toes on a slack day.

It was clear my audience was no longer numberless nor should be after all though its members might be polite enough to say they heard me even agreed and conceded that I was brilliant but I had to admit it was either their memory of faded times or outright lies to save me the humiliation of the truth and in truth I haven't the words anymore have for certain not the capacity or even the aspiration to project the news or be a recipient of the tributes or the praise know not whether I should be caring that I have not.

They come to me in greatly diminished frequency and numbers now both the words and the people not so much followers as bystanders and they have come to expect much less of me for I can communicate even less than when I could mouth the words make at least the motions for that too has stopped nor can I even write or distill with any coherence my thoughts.

There is no script no words and what goes on in my brain for something does cannot be described but even these stray reflections are fading the dream flourishes ending and I am tumbling towards a forgotten state which leaves me to retreat from all and everyone and broadcast for the record my echoing silence.

Pay Dirt

The grimy station wagon just pulled into Vegas after the drive from California and this time it was Mommy, not Daddy or the kids, that needed the bathroom, so when they hit the Slot-Slot Gas Station, she was doubly thrilled. Sitting on the potty to pee, she was surprised to find three slot machines all within easy reach from her seated position. She took some rolls of quarters out of her bag and started dropping and cranking. What a perfect introduction to gambling. This was what they came to Vegas for, and she hadn't expected such privacy. She did have to breathe through her mouth to avoid the stench, and the dust from the floor felt like it was creeping up her legs. But these were small inconveniences. After a while, Daddy knocked on the door and asked her what was holding things up. They had to check into the hotel by six and had a ways to go. She told him she was sick and just to let her be for a while. Just when she was about depleted (of coins, that is) she'd win ten or fifty quarters. For her, this was as romantic as if she were throwing the coins in the Trevi fountain, with each small win a dream come true. Ricky knocked on the door next, telling her that Daddy was getting impatient and that she had better hurry up. "Tell your Daddy, it's not a pretty sight in here and he should be thankful we found this place or would he like me to do it in the car?" Mommy went from one machine to the next, never giving up her potty seat. She even got used to the smell. Little Danielle shouted through the door, "Daddy said that if you don't come out in five minutes, he's going to leave without you." "You can tell your father I am an ailing woman, cleansing my system, and the Lord will deal with him if he abandons me here." She had dropped her last quarter. It went nowhere and she was fifty dollars poorer. As she stood up, she heard her husband's voice shouting over the car's engine, "Then walk it, bitch." She washed the gray residue of quarters from her hands, finally got her you know what out of there and shielding her eyes from the harsh Nevada sun, mumbled, "The bastard actually left." She kicked the parched ground and dirty sand hit a white stretch limousine filling up with regular unleaded. She knocked on its tinted window and asked the kindly looking grey haired passenger if she could borrow fifty dollars or so in quarters to make a telephone call. He told her he was sure they could work something out. She went into that car and they drove around for five days. She was dropped off back at the Slot-Slot Gas Station's Ladies' Room, wearing a gaudy sequined red dress and spiky heels and carrying a red glittering purse. She freshened up, applying thickly caked makeup, red nail polish, red lipstick. In a few seconds, a patina of dust dulled the red shine of her shoes. She paid no mind to the slot machines this time. There was a heavy knocking and her husband's voice, "You done yet, tramp, we're heading back home." "You bet", she said, opening the door, and nearly knocking him over with her flaming crimson aura.

pillow fight

warding off insomnia, i was having a pillow fight with myself in the bedroom of a large hotel suite, throwing the feather filled sacks across a king-sized bed, from one side of the room to the other, sometimes jumping up on the bed, trying to hit myself by running impossibly to the spot where i was hurling the pillows a moment after lofting them and invariably missing myself and having to pick the pillows up off the floor and fluff them up for the next round, but not very often since there were dozens of pillows, as i customarily requested. in my defensive capacity, of course, i wouldn't want to be hit, but i'd still have to make a good faith effort to get close to being hit, making it appear that but for an expert dodge that saved me by a breath, i would have had to concede the point. otherwise, where would be the challenge?

it was not a very rewarding game. i could of course have grabbed the pillows by the corners of their cases and beat myself on the back with them, but self-flagellation was not the object. it was precision and good wholesome fun, so i kept trying. i threw in slow motion and ran at top speed to where i had aimed and actually, once or twice (by this time it would have been near dawn), when i had lofted the pillow up so it nearly reached the ceiling, i managed to hit my target, myself that is, as it fell in a nearly vertical downward path. i was quite bleary eyed by then and was anticipating with little eagerness my 6 AM wakeup call.

i didn't really want to beat myself, nor did i want to be beaten by myself, and how could i objectively even decide which one of me was on which side, or when? it was a workout, i had to admit, and in my exhaustion from running back and forth, i gave up trying to decide on a winner and loser, let alone a score, and plopped on the bed with one of the pillows, clutching it umbilically. i declared a truce, which was the only sensible outcome. the fight would be a draw and i was entitled to reconstitute myself and sleep, which i finally could, for ten minutes before the wake-up call wished me good morning and hoped i had had a restful evening. i answered that we had, not that anyone on the taped message heard me, not that anyone at all heard me, except myself, but that was all that counted.

Political Aspirations

On TV the other night, I thought I was watching the new president in front of a convenience store giving a speech on his health care agenda, but soon realized it had to be the old president, especially since a demonstrator held up a sign that said *Fraud*. But then, as he continued, out of breath and with heaving chest, pontificating through a mouthful of stained and decayed teeth, he seemed to look more like the old president's wife. Of course, it couldn't have been her because, though hale, hearty and horny, she suffered a heart attack and died three years ago, while in flagrante delicto with the current attorney general, who had been retained from the previous administration and was also, therefore, the old attorney general, though potbellied and bald by now. To show his gratitude for the new appointment, he became intimate with the new president's first lady, which was quite acceptable to the new chief of state, who had his own affairs to attend to. Pretty soon, all the presidents, present and past, had assembled, most of them chalky and in various states of putrefaction. It was hard to tell one from another, and it made no sense for me to continue trying to identify that first speechifier. I was starting, by this point, not to feel quite like myself. In answer to a question posed by the newscaster, the presidents concurred that it would be a smashing idea, get this, for little old me, to run for president. It was a thrill, indeed, to hear my name spoken on TV. But I never had political ambitions, and I said as much to the screen, as if I were speaking to them all in person, and that I would rather just assassinate a presidential hopeful, and elope with his wife, if the spry old attorney general didn't beat me to the punch. They must have heard me for they looked me in the eye and cheered. Maybe, just maybe, whoever takes over the helm of the government (presumably not the candidate I assassinated) could consider appointing me as attorney general for a change. I have been told I bear some resemblance to the current one, or at least to his long neglected wife. And regardless of how things work out, I can assure my colleagues that as much as I might kiss, I won't tell.

The Prunes' Revenge

They were moist, silent, the 3 of them, as I took them out of the new bag. There was no complaint as I set them on the cutting board, slicing and chopping, nor as I tossed them into the pot of water I set to boil in preparation for adding oatmeal. But as I distractedly watched the water just begin to bubble, they began flapping about, indecorously at that, and spoke simultaneously, "Hey, what do you think you're doing? We're simply boiling down here. You should only choke on your oatmeal (and us). What did we ever do to you?" I told them I'd been mixing diced prunes into my oatmeal for years. They kept up their grumbling and rambling but as the water roiled, their speech slowed, and grew garbled. One by one, they began to quiet down and succumb but for the largest chunk, slurring, "Have you no decency, sir?" imputing to me, I'm sure it meant to insinuate, a character not unlike Joe McCarthy's. I threw in the oatmeal, drowning them all out, and stirred occasionally. After 4 minutes, I added a tablespoon of honey, blending it in well, and transferred the contents to a bowl, sprinkling a teaspoon of flax seed on top. Unable to avert my gaze from the bowl, I felt as if the bits of prune were eyes staring at me accusingly. This didn't stop me from digging in but I swore I could hear their voices reverberating in my belly and could feel their revenge starting to work.

pursuit

after we broke up, i wondered, given the way she had described her last boyfriend as "vigorously pursuing" her, how she would characterize me to her next one because my account, if anyone asked, would be that we merely happened upon each other and decided to make a go of it.

it's true i may have turned a trifle more eager, though after a year she was still no closer to me, and less inclined than ever to reciprocate my tepid overtures, but one could never say i pursued her with anything approaching vigor, and at the end, we just drifted apart.

now i wonder whether the pencil sketch i drew of her still hangs over the white leather sofa in her sunroom, and whether she thinks of me when she looks at it and fancies, perhaps, that i, too, courted her relentlessly and will say as much to her new boyfriend when he asks her about it.

or maybe she doesn't feel the need to justify the sketch or discuss us at all with him, and maybe one day, sipping martinis on her roof, they will fold it into a paper airplane, release it

THE SAD PARADE

and, as it descends through the dusk, will dreamily watch, the same way she and i would lean forward against the chin high brick wall, swirling our drinks, and be transfixed by flocks of gliding blackbirds, a pursuit we gathered to be singularly our own, except so little is singular these days, and we, all of us, are fated to give in to inclinations we once had regardless of what fictions they may summon.

the sad parade of big candles

marching in daylight, wasting their drama, they wind throughout the city, adding nothing to the mid-day sun. tall tapered figures struggling to show the spectators it doesn't matter whether their light illuminates or not. creamy candles out of step with each other, faltering but unable to stop or they'll be stuck to the spot from their drippings. flickering is their way of waving the hand, the derby, the flag. and the crowd, despite being unimpressed, courteously signals back with waves, winks, and thumbs up, cheering them on. but the candles' timing is all off and their dubious pride fools no one. they are ashamed - that they are sluggish, that they are melting and shrinking, unsynchronized, and are no longer the smooth vertical rods they once were. they are ashamed that night is falling and it seems they won't make it. the end comes even sooner with an unexpected onset of nimbostratus clouds and showers which were not in the forecast and which the parade marshal did not expect nor take precautions against. through every quarter of the city are heard faint fizzlings of dampened wicks, are seen little puffs of smoke above stumpy wax-dribbled stems, eerie in twilight's onset, and the wind comes on strong, here and there kicking over the little nubbins no longer visible. when nightfall is complete, the moon, sympathetic, hides her face, and the gas lamps extinguish themselves as does the rest of creation, out of respect.

Sick of it All

You said he said she said she was sick. She said she was sick of it all, all the attention. She said she was stifled by his attentiveness, to her. But I have trouble believing this, for she is not a person to reject attention. On the contrary, she craves it. Now if you would have me believe he told you she actually said as much, and she really believed what she was saying herself, that she was sick and tired of all his consideration (and mind you I myself can attest that he glommed onto her), why, I might very well eat my hat, and then you'd really see somebody sick because I do not even own a hat, and my hair, I might add, not that I'm proud of it, has not been washed for three years (this because of the priority I have given to world affairs over personal hygiene), but rest assured I do not boast idly about eating a hat as if it were an empty expression. To show my earnestness, I would order one, and in the meanwhile grab for one that isn't there on my head, pulling out instead the poisonous mushrooms growing in my hair and licking my fingers clean of them, sacrificing myself that is, although I hope to have a physician nearby to administer the antidote. And this is probably exactly the kind of thing that happened to her, that is some self-inflicted injury not at all brought on by his over solicitousness but by her wanting to lay the blame on someone else's doorstep despite her affection for him, and because of the taboo on self-mutilation, and since she never let on that she was fond of his attentions, in fact outright told him, lying through her teeth, that they infuriated her, he gradually withdrew them and this hurt her more than all the world. More than likely this is the simplest explanation for the mysterious rash of afflictions surrounding us. You yourself, I might add, have not been looking at all well lately. Could it be something in the air?

A Sizeable Confrontation

An obese man, morbidly so, uneasy about his clumsy gait but proud of taking guff from no one, wobbles down the sidewalk, stung, he can feel, by penetrating stares. He stops, turns around. In an instant, their eyes are diverted. He continues cautiously, and again, intently, they survey his bulk, he has no doubt. He stops, turns around again. They have taken poses. A man roots through his wallet. Another, hands behind his back, scrutinizes the overcast sky and whistles. A third snaps his fingers to a headset's beat infusing his ears. A woman scrunches up her face, distressed over God knows what. A teenage couple gazes intently into each other's eyes but he sees the girl sneak a passing peek at him. His face reddens and he stamps his foot on the ground, a feat in itself. He shouts to them all, "I know who you are and I know what you are doing, so just stop playing your games." They drop their facades and stare at him blatantly, as if he's a freak. He lets down his own guise, cowers, as they come closer from all quadrants, taking in his enormity, poking his belly and thighs to convince themselves that he is real. He tries to hunch over to protect himself, but there is no way he can compress his bulk. He cries, "Please, I didn't mean it." "Oh yes you did," they accuse him, "you most certainly did." Humiliated, he deflates to the size of a pin head as his accusers merge into a massive donut of humanity and loom over him threateningly.

Sojourn to the Deep

Tired of getting nowhere on the skin of this world, I stepped off the ferry or pier, or jumped from the boat, into the blue sea foam and, no swimmer, got as far as my blessings would take me, then succumbed to multiple deliria floating up from the sunken bottom, these confusions fermenting within me and fomenting myriad suggestible visions that had been pitifully absent in my inert addiction to atmosphere where I too easily gave in to life.

Nodding approval to my fate as if I knew, as if I could even breathe, must have seemed bizarre to the marine ephemera looking on. But I found, underwater, the most morphable white anemones never touched by wind and such breathtaking intangible diversions that I nearly gave up the ghost, or so it felt at first, before going further for a sunken bobbin I spied in the deep, when I could have devoted my energy to ascending for air. The sparkle of the golden yarn was worth more than any claim to life. I saw miracles pulled from coral like rabbits from a top hat or emerging like fish from a water logged boot.

Uninterrupted, unending, and unprotected immersion troubles nonetheless though consciousness does not disolve so quickly. Flailing but not in fear, I let myself be drawn down a liquid trail, mesmerized along each unconnected stepstone to eternity. Throwing a seaweed satchel over my shoulder, I rummaged in the blue forest of ever-midnight, and set no anchors, flush with the excitement of forgetting my already ancient origins. There was no end to my sinking as Neptune answered my prayers and I was tangled in a net of dredged up memory and stunned into a simulacrum of life. Bewildered by visions of old surroundings, familiar but indecipherable, I was propelled to the surface, where I coughed, cleared my lungs, was in wonder at my returning pulse, and lay on my back on the beach where I still remain, soaking in the sojourn as if I were still below the surface.

South Jersey, Pine Barrens

The Park Ranger at the Visitor Center said the Nature Tour would start at 3 PM from the Nature Center at the east end of The Village, as the visitor complex was called, and as there were only 5 minutes to spare, I headed off, without delay, in the direction he pointed, but the arrows led me only to a shaky looking building with scaffolding, marked Nature Pavilion. No one else was waiting for a tour, or for anything, for that matter, so at 5 past 3 I left and went back to the Visitor Center.

There I complained to the Park Ranger who asked whether I went to the old Nature Center or the new Nature Center and when I described it he said, "No, no, no, that was the Old Nature Center. Take this map. Do you see Building 38 on the west end? That's the New Nature Center." Certain I would never catch the group, I hurried off anyway to a small cedar cabin that said Nature Center, plain and simple. It was 3:30. A short young man with a head of dark curly moss like hair asked if I needed help, and I said, "Yes, is there still time to catch the group that went on the 3 PM tour?" He told me he was the guide and since I was the only one to show up, we might as well get started, so we headed for the Lake, the Old Lake, he

THE SAD PARADE

was careful to point out, where he began to explain the use of canoes. "But isn't this a walking tour?" I demanded to know. I couldn't swim and looked askance at the canoe.

By now it was 3:45. "Oh, the Walking Nature Tour was leaving from the New Nature Center. I lead the 3 PM Canoe Nature Tour." "Now, wait a minute", I said, "I thought your cabin was the New Nature Center, Building 38. The Park Ranger told me exactly how to get here." "No, no, no," said the canoe leader, "those numbers are meaningless. The Park Ranger misinformed you. He must be the New Park Ranger. The Old Park Ranger would have known better. There is a building on the east end of the Village marked Nature Pavilion. That was the site of the Old Nature Center. My cabin is only the temporary New Nature Center, until they finish renovating the Nature Pavilion. It will become the new New Nature Center. In fact, we are calling it the New Nature Center already, and calling my cabin the Old Nature Center. Granted, the naming is a bit premature, but we don't get lost too often. Anybody who's been here awhile can set you straight."

"But I was there already. There weren't any people. I waited." "Yes," the canoe leader continued, "I understand. In fact the Walking Nature Tour leader phoned me to say he was moving the starting time to 3:30 in case stragglers like yourself came late. He was probably at the canteen having some coffee. "Look," I continued, "can I possibly catch them? I've been looking forward to learning about this area and I really don't like boating." "If you hop in, we just might find them. They should be foraging around that stand of pine just around the lake's bend."

I overcame my phobia and hopped in the canoe. Within a matter of minutes, we approached the shore and could see the Walking Tour group. There were a goodly number of people, naked, snaking between the trees, and picking mushrooms. I had feared this. It was another of those nude fungus frolics and I wasn't going to waste my time on one more of them. "Listen," I said to the Canoe Nature Tour Leader, "I changed my mind. And I'm sure I can get used to the canoe. Would you give me a nature tour of the Lake?" "The Old Lake or the New Lake?" he asked.

Shoe - Fly, Don't Bother Me

The weaselly shoe store sales clerk told me the 10 would be a better fit but I insisted that I was a 10 ½. He tried to convince me against the larger size but I wouldn't relent. Finally, he threw up his hands and said with a tinge of insolence that if I felt so strongly about it, I might as well go with my instincts, so I took the 10 ½. "Well, I showed him!" I thought, as I paid and strutted home with the pair, boxed and under my arm.

But frankly, I found myself swimming in the larger size. When I attempted to return them, this same clerk, Hymie, by the tag on his lapel (although I'd lay odds it was an assumed name) snickered and reminded me of how he had urged me to take the 10 to begin with and that the time for returns had expired. It was, you see, 3 years since I'd bought them. An expert in formulating bogus excuses to save my hide, I explained that my primary reason for bringing them back was that the interiors were not watertight. Thus, whenever I drank wine from either of them, as was my habit with dinner, it leaked from the inside edge of the mid-sole. I was sure he could resell them to a tee-totaler. He brushed off my justification as a "feeble excuse." As you can imagine, I was not pleased with his attitude. I pointed to the shoes, which I happened to be wearing at the time, to show him that, but for the leakage issue, they were as good as new, and well broken in to boot. I had kept them polished with my own blend of carnauba wax and squid ink and built up the worn heels with a proprietary rubber formulation of latex sap I personally harvested from fig trees in Malaysia.

A sneer formed on his face as he called the manager, Mr. Foote, who came over promptly. Looking down and, seeming to address the shoes more than either Hymie or me, he intoned, "What seems to be the trouble here?" I presented my ironclad case and rested my defense. All the lowly clerk could sheepishly add was, "But I did ask him to take a 10, sir." "Asked him?" Mr. Foote repeated angrily, the toes of his bare feet wiggling up and down as if in anticipation of something grand. "How many times have I told you, Hymie, you must consult with me when there are disputes about size?" He examined my shoes closely and I invited him to try them on, which he did, without bothering to put on any socks. Distinctly pleasurable quivers radiated up and down his body. He'd never tried on a pair as comfortable and handsome looking, he confessed, and asked me to set my price and he'd buy them back. I told him all I wanted was to recover my original cost. Mr. Foote happily agreed and to top it off he gave me 2 new pairs of size 10s and the keys to the store after he fired Hymie. To show my appreciation, I asked him to join me for a beer. "Very kind of you, sir, but I don't drink," he shyly disclosed.

The Superfluity of Wings

After much deliberation, I decided, just the other day, to forego my steadfast companions, my wings, that is, and fly unencumbered. *Beautifully liberating* is the phrase that first came to mind, and then the word, *exhilarating*. I had been hopeful that if I was determined, it would be possible. I waited for a strong updraft and there I was, as if it were the most natural thing in the world, taking off, soaring, circling, swooping down, spiraling up, seeing the world from not all that different a perspective but feeling lighter, clearer headed and in awe of everything, even myself, divorced from those masses of white feathers. I had been grateful for them, no doubt, for they had lofted me to greater heights than I knew possible when I assumed they were indispensable. It may have been my imagination but it looked as though the tiny people below were cheering me on. I knew I could not rely on the invigorating wind indefinitely. Not wanting to press my luck too much by trying to stay up exclusively on my own power, and knowing I'd have other chances, I settled into a downdraft. As the wind let up and I lost more altitude, I gave in to gravity only as much as safety demanded and, softly enough not to injure anything except perhaps my pride, I landed, bottom first, on the two massive wings I had left hibernating atop the giant sand dune a scant few minutes ago.

Taking a Dump in the Middle of the Night

I was squirming like crazy and didn't know if it was real or the dream I was in but I sure had to go bad. I was in a classroom full of these weird looking kids with bulging eyes and antennas popping out of their foreheads and we were in the middle of a very long test and the teacher said we had one and one-half hours to complete section three and we couldn't leave the room early, not for any reason, until the last person had completed it and even though these kids were probably from outer space maybe even a more intelligent life form they still looked dumb and I was practically doubled over when the guy next to me whispered, with a British accent yet, "It ain't that 'ard, bloke."

But what did he know about it. It was damn hard. The test and my intestines, both. I had no idea why I was taking the crazy test. It was just torture. Section three looked like geometry. There were all these triangles and other shapes and numbers and I had to say what were the lengths of the sides and the sizes of the angles but, pressing my hand on my belly, I didn't know if I could hold it in. Then out of the blue there was a question about General George Custer. A mistake? Who cares? I felt better for a second because I figured I knew the answer especially if it had to do with the Little Big Horn because I had been at the battle myself but it turned out the choices to the question were all numbers and I hate numbers. Dates, how many wounded, latitudes and longitudes, rounds of ammunition fired, and that kind of thing. "What idiocy," I thought, as I looked at my watch and saw only ten minutes gone by since I started section three.

Then this girl on the other side of me, she had these boobs shaped like kitchen funnels which she kept squishing maybe to convince me that they were real, well she poked me and asked "Do you smell something bad?" and I thought "Oh, no, if she gives me one more poke like that it's all gonna come tumbling out." I thought maybe if I raised my hand real meekly the teacher would make an exception, I mean to let me go to the bathroom if I promised I wouldn't look up the answers in the hallway or talk to anybody or make fun of the weird kids and I'd be back real quick. But she didn't even look up. I think maybe she fell asleep. That was my chance.

I took off my shoes and walked slowly and ultra-quietly up the aisle but the door wouldn't open and the brass knob made a loud click as if came off in my hand. The whole class looked at me, their antennas bobbing like those fake ones made of springs that they sell on the street but these were, let's just say hard wired. If that didn't scare the, well you know what, out of me I don't know what did. I woke up and took this wicked dump that reached so high it touched my you know what.

I was so relieved I fell back asleep right there on the bowl picking up my dream where it left off. The test had ended. The teacher was wide awake again. She gave me a certificate of achievement, I could only guess for what. I was leaving the room proudly when I realized I didn't have my pants on and the she said, "Just one thing, Wexler, before you leave the room, be sure to wipe your ..." and she paused. "I know what," I said.

Taking Stock

Under instructions from the Commissioner, the woman in rhinestone sunglasses speaking in Dutch accented English, and carrying a clipboard, was going from office to office with an alphabetized list of first names starting with A, B, C, D and E, and interrogating each worker in private about the co-worker next on the list. Thus, she started by asking Annabel questions about Arnie, then planned to proceed to Billy to enquire about Bobby, and continue down the names until after two dozen or so workers she would get to Ezra whom she would ask to confirm or dispute certain reputed facts about Annabel, thus returning full circle. The Dutch, or maybe German, woman questioned Annabel in halting English, and when the latter said she was fluent in Dutch and would be happy to converse in it, the woman continued in English with a French accent. When Annabel asked to see the full list of names, the woman drew the clipboard to her chest and said it was confidential and, besides, she had only been assigned A-E.

Annabel knew this must be some kind of ruse since she herself had already been interviewed by the Commissioner in person as part of his own A-E check earlier in the year, and when Annabel told her as much, the sun-glassed woman, switching to a thick Russian accent, pleaded not to be turned in as her back and groin were already badly bruised from her last encounter with the Commissioner and she was still in her childbearing years. As for Billy and Bobby, they overheard everything from their shared office under Annabel's desk, and knew equally well that something funny was afoot since the Vice-Commissioner had confronted them just the other day as part of the A-E interrogation. What they hadn't realized was that it was, in fact, Annabel, disguised as the Vice-Commissioner, who had been down there and riskily defying protocol altogether not only by interviewing them jointly but recording it all. Billy and Bobby denied each other's accusations and harsh words flowed freely. She knew, as well, that she was jeopardizing her own career and her on-again off-again relationship, semi-sleazy as it was, with the Commissioner by this act of sabotage, but she was fed up with Billy and Bobby, worthless slime balls that they were. She hoped that once the Commissioner was presented with the contradictions between her findings and his own, he would applaud her initiative and she could cement her relationship with him once and for all. Further, it might offer the evidence needed to evict the squatters from the prime real estate under her desk But now, complicating everything, this woman of 1001 accents made her unwelcome appearance. It was just getting to be too much for Annabel.

The woman, momentarily removing her rhinestone sunglasses to rub her eyes, tried in accents of Irish, Swedish, and Italian, to convince Annabel that she was prepared to give up the whole business, as long as Annabel would not betray her. It was true she had taken it upon herself to redo, without the Commissioner's knowledge, his A-E queries, to put herself back in his good graces because she, like Annabel, was expecting to discover some discrepancies with his conclusions, and not just regarding Billy and Bobby. At one time, she too had been his favorite, spellbound as he was with her uncanny ability to simulate the accents of natives of other countries during their steamy assignations before, of course, she was supplanted by Annabel. But now the game was up and all the woman wanted was to escape with her life. Annabel told her not to worry. She wouldn't turn her in to the Commissioner before the morning. Annabel also had in mind to inform on Billy and Bobby on some trumped up charge, like their licking her ankles without asking first. The truth was they always did ask and she always consented. And she might as well report them for looking up her skirt practically every day, though given the location of their office, it was hard to avoid, and she rather encouraged it. Indeed, now there might be a legitimate excuse for a reconciliation with the Commissioner, long overdue.

As for this possibly foreign woman, Annabel offered to give her a nice massage and take care of all those troublesome, meddlesome, letters that were spoiling everything for everybody. This was just what the woman was hoping for. It was time to face up to the fact that the Commissioner had tired of her. The tears she seemed to be shedding, which broke Annabel's heart, were really no more than tiny rhinestones popping out of her sunglass frames. Keeping the glasses on, she let her clothing and clipboard drop. Annabel gently kneaded her neck and back, causing her to moan pleasurably in a wordless accent redolent of Japanese, half faded peonies, and steaming miso soup. The Commissioner, watching it all on closed circuit with his new concubine, ZzaZza, was pleased to see in what high regard he was held by his underlings.

Teaching the Trapezoid a Lesson

Believe me, I didn't start it. The stupid shape kept blabbering and blathering like there was no tomorrow, and I aimed to guarantee it would have no future indeed, if it didn't put an end to the meaningless chatter. "Hold your tongue," I said, or I'll bisect you, trisect you, intersect you, and vivisect you." But the trapezoid was constitutionally incapable of keeping its trap shut. And there it went, swinging at me, missing, it's true, but hell bent on mischief. What could I do but, in self-defense, punch back? And so, our rumble started.

I grabbed it by an acute angle, swung it like a lasso, and released it like a discus into the darkening sky. I could hear it faintly crying, "Sorry, I'm so sorry," slyly trying to convince me to forgive it its trespasses and assume the guilt myself. But I was free of fault, and it was too late for that game. I wasn't buying. The trapezoid found itself imprisoned in the dense branches of a tree, with no hope of escape. That's where it learned the hard lessons of humility and quiet. I listened attentively to its silence.

THE SAD PARADE

Convinced by this time that it had atoned, I set it free with pruning shears, and put it upon the creek where it drifted downstream, and I upon it, keeping the trapezoid in check and, with nary a further word spoken, the two of us on the lookout for other shapes to educate.

Time will Tell

Our engagement started to feel, even to me, as if it were dragging on interminably but I had only my procrastination to blame for the delay. Reproached whenever I looked at my fiancée for some sign of forgiveness, I was met with impatiently circling hands and a pale face which by its very inscrutability was a rebuttal to all my pleas of patience. Every day, on cue, I was reminded with alarm about how fleeting time was and how we were not getting any younger. So, with too much weakness in my resistance to shore it up, I went ahead and married the beautiful wind-up deco desk clock encased in solid mahogany. Transfixed by those slim golden hands sweeping across the elongated black Roman numerals marking the seconds, minutes, and hours, I gave in, and since then have been consistently punctual in my comings and goings. Mixed marriage though it was, we reconciled our minor differences and lived harmoniously. Our progeny – 1, 2, 3 – arrived like clockwork and brought us timeless joy. Now, in the twilight of our years, we know we could have done no better, sealing our betrothal as we did, in opposition to the critical eyes who scoffed that we would never synchronize our differences. We are content in our momentary eternity, blissfully ticking away. We have never looked back and continue to traverse the winding road we set out upon so long ago.

To Prepare Broth First Chop Bone

Or so the recipe said which was why the man at the butcher block counter was chopping a wooly mammoth bone and its marrow with a hefty knife that had never been honed and was very old and rusty making it tough to chop into ever smaller pieces flying every which way to be gathered and cut again and again and it was a very big bone he kept chopping and got into a rhythm till it was all gone all powder all dust but he went right on chopping the wooden chopping block till it too was dust and the knife by now since this went on for who knows how many months resembled a crowbar and he went on beating and banging till the oak counter gave way and he smothered every last fragment into indivisible particles and fell to his knees and pounded through the linoleum and onto the floor boards and when the misshapen lump of metal that had been the knife shattered he kicked it away, made two big fists and pounded some more before he realized he had decimated the recipe and had no idea what the next steps were to make the broth and with his guests waiting uncomfortably at the dining room table for 2 years, he announced that there would a change in the menu and ordered pizza to the delight of everyone still conscious.

To Such an End

Your small wrists always kept busy, whatever you did. Your small occupied hands, wrists sewing and knotting and knitting, painting, digging and planting, more out of less, wholes from pieces, creating, filling empty spaces with your handiwork. Your delicate hands, fingers, wrists wrists did not rest, preparing the food, setting the table, distributing the glasses, pouring the water and wine. I loved those hands and their actions - brushing hair out of children's eyes, petting the dog, scratching backs with red shiny, nails, or when they were clasped in prayer. Your intense fingers were smack on the project, always on the move, skimming over the piano, the harp, lacing children's shoes, arranging your skirt. Sometimes your hands looked completely separate from you as at the concert, nails maybe pink this time, gold bracelets on wrists, clapping with enthusiastic applause like a distinct life form evolved with no near relatives, your fine narrow hands as expressive as your face, no, more expressive, even than your eyes. I want so badly to hold them, entwine your fingers with mine, caress your wrists again, but there you went and slit them and it was such a shame.

The Third Wife

The first two I lost track of. I misplaced them, somewhere between Rochester and Poughkeepsie. The third I kept in the oversized top drawer of the bureau, which had originally been occupied by photographs I had taken of her in her younger years before she turned portly. These were intermingled with snapshots of wives one and two. It has been years, though, since I donated the photographs to the thrift shop down the street. They sold briskly to the steady customer in the black rain coat, I was told.

The third wife's ample frame made it necessary for me to leave the drawer partly open. I fed her chocolate éclairs each morning, and would crawl in with her, as best I could, on Friday and Tuesday evenings, briefly, of course, for neither one of us wanted to overextend the amorous interludes. She was grateful that I always remembered, at bedtime, to drape the bureau with an oversized blanket patterned with pink and gray bunnies, to keep her out of drafts. My main motivation, though, was to avoid inadvertently looking at her.

She made me swear to seal it upon her death, to make it her coffin. She didn't care whether I buried it or not. I thought I might send it out to sea, but decided that such a burial would disrespect her landlubber inclinations. Once I heard her crying. She blamed loneliness. I bought her a pet rabbit, and from what I could tell, they seemed snug and happy. With the animal's presence, my visits became less frequent, for it offered at least as much companionship as I could. However, with her ever increasing bulk, she crowded even the rabbit.

One morning I found the bureau overturned and her sprawled on the silk gold Persian rug patterned with pomegranates. She seemed unharmed although I could not vouchsafe the same for the rabbit, whose tail peered out from under her corpulent belly. On the floor, just within arm's reach, I left her a package of eight eclairs. I could sense, by her strained stretching towards them, just how much she appreciated my gesture. It was, one could say, a parting gift, for I just had to get away for a week. I packed my bags for Syracuse to see if I could track down either of my first two wives.

Utterly

My darling i saw your lipstick in the supermarket - and it was pink like the fairyland of spinning carousels - and i said could i introduce myself to you - i said to myself - and you heard it every blessed word of it and said surely - as you kissed me and i felt the lipstick pink implant itself on my lips - therefore i thought it was just endlessly remarkable that our lips would ever - who ever would have thought - there among the jalapeno peppers and the kiwis overpriced as always - would have thought - not myself surely not me - that there would have been a chance - and shoppers from far out in the frozen juice section were coming to watch - and we had no shame - no concern that anyone - the store manager in his grim denim apron notwithstanding - that not a single one of them would intervene - and it was all so heavenly with the fluorescents and the coolness of the mega air conditioning units - even the shopping carts began swaying - and while housewives tore off their blouses in ecstatic celebration and a show of confidence in our union we glided along the speckled grey linoleum past the jumbo eggs down aisle seven with the canned whole tomatoes to the express checkout line and they all - every one of the customers made way - the sea parted and although we were still firmly glued together and did not say a word they knew we meant to say "do you mind?" as we forged ahead forsaking at the last moment our shopping carts, our goods unpurchased and no longer even desired - and the checkout girl didn't miss a beat chewing her bubble gum as she motioned us on through – just as well – we were love rich but money poor and they never would have accepted our checks – but you my darling, and i, we accepted each other, much more than accepted, and who could want more? – so, just before whooshing through the automatic doors, i nabbed or should i say stole a gift for you alone, a bouquet of coral roses, or was it cotton candy? – seeing you blush, i could barely keep my balance - and you knew enough not to ask where we were headed, what we were running towards - no i would not have to get the car - there was no car - never had been - the parking lot was quite empty but that sky was such a sensual pink and filled with such strange and colorful sea birds here far from any water that we were caught in the upsweep, utterly unimaginable, indecipherable, but real, and never looked back again.

The Way of the Rodeo

In her cowgirl hat silver belt banners twirl high carved leather boots with stars and bits of red plastic her lasso and pistol shots ring out the bandstand hushed anticipating as she goes for the bull nostrils flaring to pull it down right on target rope settles around massive black neck with the grace of pearl necklace bestowed upon bristling Ethiopian monarch by adoring slave still the fight that stubborn resistance refusing to yield to beauty at last seems beaten roped and the tumultuous cheers hats thrown high but unruly beast once more takes strength insists on his own way tossing bulk around with fury making last stab at intransigence and she a slight girl her eyes sparkling moist holds tight uses kind words gentle tugs and pulls in a docile animal with the sweetest of whispers so he'd be lapping milk from her palms.

Wedding

The shelter of the wedding and the wooden beams. The half-moon hanging over the clipped trees. The passion flowers lining the entrance. Music filtering to the garden. Lace and satin wait for the couple. Hotel dreams of the honeymoon. Giggling chambermaids pirouette and sing. Pastry morsels set out for the birds. Stars and comets flashing through clouds. The hesitating action of eyelashes gives way to the fusion of eyes. Fireworks in the meeting of tongues. Windows clutching bouquets thrown high.

Wedding Bells

The chair unexpectedly proposed to the table lamp, taking even the chair himself by surprise, considering the lengthy courtship, the chair's fear that he would be rebuffed, and his unease about the lamp's tendency to sit on things, other than the chair. The chair shifted away from the sofa and angled himself toward the lamp. He asked her indulgence for he had something momentous to say. When the words spilled out the lamp turned on and off to make sure she wasn't dreaming. The chair, 19th century walnut, a curlicued back, possessed a formal but inviting seat upholstered in gold and green stripes, conforming but not plush. The lamp had a pale peach ruffled shade and Greek style amphora base with a frieze of an Athenian maiden in different running poses. On one side the maiden's banner read, "I will. I will." On the other, with a chorus, she asked "Do you love me?" The chair rocked back and forth, spun on one leg, and said, "I'm yours. Be mine." So she threw discretion to the wind and snuggled into his seat, his lap in fact, and cast a wide circle of light. He gallantly stepped her over an imaginary threshold. She glowed with love and bathed him in it. In unison, throughout the house, kitchen timers, clock radios, doorbells, telephones, and smoke alarm detectors went off in celebration.

We Recover Lampshades

So the sign in the window of the lighting store announced. My first guileless thought was, "Why? Are they lost?" No sooner did I realize my mistake, than I determined that maybe I shouldn't rule out my first impression after all. I had no lampshade needing a new skin, but remembered one that had gone missing.

Opening the door set off a jingling bell. The shopkeeper, surrounded by hundreds of lamps in a stiflingly tiny space, was small, smelly, and unshaven. I told him of a shade I'd had years ago, widely flaring, pleated, cream colored, and embedded with golden flecks. It was the lesser used, at least recently, of the lamps on my bed's two end tables and, one morning, three years ago, was simply gone. It was the favorite of the girlfriend I had dumped about the same time. Could he help?

He scratched the stubble on his chin, took an old, dusty, looseleaf binder from the bookshelf, flipped through black and white photographs preserved in plastic, and stopped near the end. He pointed to one of a lampshade remarkably similar, sitting, like a hat, on the head of a woman looking remarkably like my ex-girlfriend. "Like this?" he asked. "Uncanny," I answered excitedly, "can you recover it?"

He pulled at his chin and smiled, two gold incisors glinting, "Without a doubt, though it will grieve the young lady to part with it." "But I mean to have her as well," I clarified. "Yes, of course, my friend, but she won't come cheap anymore. I would suffer inconsolably to part with my wife." "I'll make it worth your while," I offered.

In accord, we shook on it, and did a little jig in celebration. We recovered our composures and returned to our respective obligations – he to retrieve my belongings and I to secure his cash.

Winner Takes All

The enemy, a vast scruffy herd of 1500 smelly and dim witted troops, is trampling our miles long rubber weaponized hose. We have stretched it far, snaked it over enemy territory in the night, maneuvered it through rocky terrain, forests, and the desert, but the enemy is wise to us, quite as we would have it. We have camouflaged it authentically enough to be taken seriously, but carelessly enough to be discovered. We have let it be known through intentional leaks that its purpose is to bring water to our parched allies. The poor feeble-minded enemy has discovered the nozzle and plugged it up in the hope of having the water back up and drown us. We have all this on good authority from our scouts, who report on enemy activity, with occasional breaks to distance themselves from the odor. So dizzily proud are the enemy at having found the nozzle that they jump up and down on the hose in a drunken revelry, resulting in innumerable small punctures from the cactus thorn spikes embedded in the soles of their boots. Once our sensors indicate that all the water has been drained, we activate an auxiliary pump to propel quick acting, permanently binding glue through the hose and allow it to dribble out the holes. They are so happy, they don't notice a thing, and continue their jumping, but each time less high because the glue is grabbing hold of them more tightly. Soon they are stuck to the hose, each and every one of the 1500. In unison they bend over to begin untangling the elaborate lacings of their boots but before they can conclude the work, a putrid stench seeps up from their years long unwashed feet and they are overcome, the lot of them. We unscrew the hose from our end and, outfitted with gas masks we charge the unconscious enemy, roll up the hose with the 1500 troops stuck to it, and encase the multi-bodied carcass in a hefty plastic container on wheels. This we have our emissaries convey, with the aid of an elephant caravan, to the highly nervous and brain-damaged enemy king, a rotten turnip if ever there was one, who is most delighted with what he refers to as the victorious return of his men, and who announces to our stupefied ears that he accepts our surrender.

About the Author

Phil Wexler has been writing poetry his entire adult life. Originally from New York City, he spent his formative years in Brooklyn before moving, as a young man, to Bethesda, Maryland, a suburb of Washington, DC.

Phil has some 170 (and growing) literary magazine publications to his credit. Although his focus has always been poetry, including prose poetry, he has dipped into the waters of fiction with several short stories. His poetry collections include The Sad Parade (Adelaide Books. 2019) and The Burning Moustache (Adelaide Books. 2020). He has organized and emceed a number of spoken word reading series over the years in the DC area. Most recently, he oversees the monthly Words out Loud at Glen Echo Park in Maryland, which includes featured readers, an open mic, and a literary trivia quiz. While in New York, his many literary haunts included the Strand Bookstore and the Unterberg Poetry Center of the 92nd Street Y and, if he just wanted a drink, there was always McSorley's Old Ale House and The White Horse Tavern. He is a longtime member of The Writer's Center in Bethesda and tries to take advantage of the DC area's vibrant literary scene there and elsewhere, such as the Politics and Prose bookstore.

Philip Wexler

Phil has edited and authored numerous book and journal technical publications in the fields of toxicology informatics and toxicology history. These include serving as Editor-in-Chief of The Encyclopedia of Toxicology, 3rd edition (2014) and Information Resources in Toxicology, 5th edition (2020), as well as series editor for a monographic series, History of Toxicology and Environmental Health, all published by Elsevier. He is also editor of Chemicals, Environment Health: A Global Management Perspective (2012. CRC Press) and co-editor-in-chief of the journal, Global Security: Health, Science and Policy (Taylor and Francis). He is a member of the US Society of Toxicology (SOT), a recipient of its Public Communications Award (2010), and a Trustee with the Toxicology Education Foundation (TEF). Phil has taught, given technical presentations, and organized public outreach events related to toxicology, internationally. After a long career of government service as a Technical Information Specialist, he retired from the Toxicology and Environmental Health Information Program of the National Library of Medicine, an arm of the National Institutes of Health, in 2018.

In addition to writing, Phil is also passionate about the arts in general and his work as a non-commercial mosaic artist. He is an avid museum- and theater-goer, and a fan of opera and Broadway musicals. Over the years, he has also been intermittently immersed in pursuits as varied as bicycle touring, hiking, fencing, indoor and outdoor gardening, and being overly attentive to he and his wife's dog, Gigi. He tries to keep up with the increasingly crazy global and domestic news and is very concerned about the state of our environment. He is married to Nancy and has one son, Jake.

www.ingramcontent.com/pod-product-compliance
Lightning Source LLC
Chambersburg PA
CBHW032231080426
42735CB00008B/808